Recasting Ritual

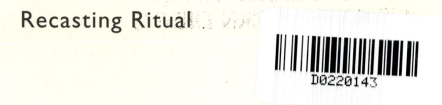

Recasting Ritual explores how ritualised action diversifies in response to varying cultural, political and physical contexts. The contributors look at how issues such as globalisation and technology affect ritual performance and how minorities often utilise performances to affirm their own identities while also speaking to outsiders.

The contributors examine the relationship between ritual meaning and social identity through case studies drawn from the Pacific, Indonesia, the Mediterranean, West Africa, Scandinavia and Latin America. Study of the theoretical underpinnings of social action affirms the independence of anthropology as a discipline distinct from cultural, media and performance studies, according it a role in elucidating contemporary and emergent human conditions.

This collection will be of interest to students of anthropology, sociology, religion and performance studies.

Felicia Hughes-Freeland is Senior Lecturer in Social Anthropology at the University of Wales Swansea. **Mary M. Crain** is Visiting Professor at the Department of Social Anthropology, University of Barcelona, Spain.

European Association of Social Anthropologists

Series facilitator: Jon P. Mitchell
University of Sussex

The European Association of Social Anthropologists (EASA) was inaugurated in January 1989, in response to a widely felt need for a professional association which would represent social anthropologists in Europe and foster cooperation and interchange in teaching and research. As Europe transforms itself in the 1990s, the EASA is dedicated to the renewal of the distinctive European tradition in social anthropology.

Other titles in the series:

Recasting Ritual

Performance, media, identity

Edited by
Felicia Hughes-Freeland and
Mary M. Crain

London and New York

First published 1998
by Routledge
11 New Fetter Lane, London EC4P 4EE

Simultaneously published in the USA and Canada
by Routledge
29 West 35th Street, New York, NY 10001

© 1998 selection and editorial matter, EASA; individual
chapters, the contributors

Typeset in Galliard by Routledge
Printed and bound in Great Britain by
T.J. International, Padstow, Cornwall

British Library Cataloguing in Publication Data
A catalogue record for this book is available from the
British Library

Library of Congress Cataloging in Publication Data
A catalogue record for this book has been requested

ISBN 0–415–18279–4 (hbk)
ISBN 0–415–18280–8 (pbk)

Contents

Contributors

Mette Bovin is Researcher at the Nordic Africa Institute, Uppsala, Sweden.

Mary M. Crain is Lecturer in Social Anthropology at the University of Barcelona, Spain.

Ingjerd Hoëm is Research Fellow at the University of Oslo, Norway.

Felicia Hughes-Freeland is Senior Lecturer in Social Anthropology at the University of Wales Swansea.

Jon P. Mitchell is Lecturer in Social Anthropology at the University of Sussex.

Ingrid Rudie is Professor of Social Anthropology at the University of Oslo, Norway.

Acknowledgements

The authors would like to thank all those who participated in the workshop 'Revising ritual: performance, media, identity' at Barcelona. A number of the papers presented there could not be included here, and we are grateful to Jon Mitchell and Mette Bovin for allowing us to include their work, which in Mette's case was written up under extreme pressure between fieldwork trips and other commitments. Her chapter provides a useful source on the WoDaaBe for those unable to read French, Danish, and so forth, and also complements the English-language films about these people. Mary M. Crain would like to thank the Generalitat de Catalunya, particularly CIRIT, and the Department of Anthropology at the University of Barcelona for providing her with the financial support which helped make this volume possible. Felicia Hughes-Freeland would like to thank the Research Committee of the University of Wales Swansea for their support in covering some of the cost of her participation at the EASA conference in Barcelona, and to the Department of Sociology and Anthropology, University of Wales Swansea, for financial assistance in preparing the manuscript for publication.

Despite global technologies such as faxes and e-mail, the process of joint editing across national boundaries remains a complex one, which is not made any easier when the diaspora of contributors is as widespread and volatile as ours has been, so we are particularly grateful to Jon Mitchell for providing sensible and soothing advice during the production of this book in his capacity as EASA series editor. Our thanks go to Manuel Delfino for his file-converting skills in Barcelona and his important help as a critical reader. We are also grateful to Al Coley, who hammered the chapters into a fit state for submission to Routledge. Finally, we would both like to thank our nearest and dearest, without whose support and patience this book would never have been completed.

Chapter 1

Introduction

Felicia Hughes-Freeland and
Mary M. Crain

Ritual is an increasingly contested and expanding arena for resistance, negotiation and the affirmation of identity. As global markets bring diverse groups into different forms of contact, so these groups strive to determine their present interests and future identities by controlling representations that range from live performance to hypermedia. Such extensions of ritual action raise important questions about the relationship of local culture to global politics, which in turn affect our understanding of the nature of groups and cultures, and the disciplinary boundaries between anthropology, media studies and performance studies.

This volume explores ritualised action, but in doing so also addresses changes in foundational anthropological paradigms for the explanation of behaviour and society. It starts from three broad questions. First, how might anthropological analyses of ritual practice respond to the diversification of performance and audience, from live to mediated contexts? Second, what can the analysis of ritual reveal about identity politics and the relationship between power and culture in global and local practices? Third, is there a future for distinctive anthropological approaches to ritualised social action, or are we set to merge into cultural, performance and media studies?

Performance, media, identity

As we were drafting this introduction, the British public was experiencing and constituting what the press referred to as 'the Diana phenomenon'. Following her death after a car accident in the early hours of 31 August 1997, 'Princess Diana' became a contested sphere. From across the world came reports and pictures of remarkable and unpredictable displays of public grief. The culmination of this week of emotion, of representations of this emotion, and the counter-representation of reason, was a funeral. This ritual was constructed from between the lines of the book of royal rules. It emerged from a process of intense negotiation, of claims and counter-claims, which produced a 'unique funeral for a unique person'. As death beatified Diana, the public pressurised the royal family and the Spencer family about the length of the procession before and after the funeral service, and the forms of access for showing their respect. If such media grieving was unprecedented, so too was the interaction between ritual, performance and media. Before our eyes was enacted the negotiation by numerous agencies, in diverse forms of representation, both of an event and of a person's posthumous identity. These forms ranged from the voices of individuals to the voice(s) of national institutions, to reflections and speculations in word and image which addressed the cause of the death, and recast its victim. This ritual process was wholly inscribed in the mesh of everyday practice, and became interwoven with it. The funeral was marked by sacrality beyond the space where it occurred – shops were closed, sporting events were cancelled – but the event marked the close of the revealing process which led up to it, and which is now yesterday's story. That performance is now over, and its rituals have been replaced by others.

Ritual is both a concept and an analytical tool, and has been given a wide range of forms and applications by anthropologists. There are three broad approaches to the analysis of ritual: first, as an event with a social function connecting the personal and the social, structurally or as anti-structure (Turner 1969); second, as an aspect of all action which is meaningful, in a processual sense (Geertz 1973); and third, as a partic-ular aspect of some action (Bell 1992). The contributors to this volume suggest that ritual is most usefully and relevantly theorised as a contested space for social action and identity politics – an arena for resistance, negotiation and affirmation. Bell's definition of ritualisation as 'a way of acting that is designed and orchestrated to distinguish and privilege what is being done in comparison to other, usually more quotidian, activities' (1992: 74) applies equally well to performance if it is not understood as the replication of a given script or text (Coleman and Elsner 1998: 48). The implication of this is that rituali-sation is best reconstructed in terms of social practices which are situated and performed (Hughes-Freeland 1998: 1).

By thinking of ritualisation, rather than ritual, we can engage with the processual aspect of ritual action. This active dimension of ritual as a performance which 'has effects on the world' and 'does things' is underscored by Gerholm (1988) and Parkin (1992: 14). Such an approach allows us to explore themes such as agency and intentionality and the interplay of creativity and constraint in social action. Instead of a ritual process which moves from one moment to another in time and space, ritualised performative practices embody creativity and constraint to be thought of as simultaneous, co-present, and co-dependent, and embodied in different forms of participation. This entails a shift in focus from form and meaning in ritual, to the different aspects of participation. It also provides insight into the analysis of spectatorship as participation. Finally, the processual approach to ritual also permits a further illuminating comparison between the unrealities of ritual and media, which helps us to think about the ways in which we frame reality/-ies and how variable framings alter our roles, our self-images, our identities.

This shifted focus is justified by the empirical circumstances of contemporary social interaction, which extend social relations beyond the spatial boundaries of a community – either face-to-face relations in a particular time and place, or the 'imagined' national community fostered by the advent of print-capitalism (Anderson 1983). The contemporary flow of populations and images within the global ecumene (Hannerz 1989) refigures both social relations and local cultural forms through a series of '-scapes' (Appadurai 1996), connections which have the potential to bring social groups into polymorphous configurations in increasingly plural or multicultural societies. Contemporary analyses of ritualised action and performance demand that we attend to the diversity of 'publics' that may be present at any particular event, delineating their specific roles and social positions. Such increasingly heterogeneous publics interpret ritualised actions in a variety of ways, often creating new dilemmas for intercultural communication and translation. Furthermore, in many instances, only certain portions of a particular society (often ethnic minorities or members of one of the dominant ethnic groups) celebrate a specific ritualised action, while other members of the society at large are ostracised from participation or assume positions or roles which may vary from 'abstention' to 'active spectator'. Ethnic and/or national minorities as well as diasporic societies utilise their own performances as arenas in which they affirm their own identities, while also speaking to 'outsiders' (see Gross *et al.* 1994). In yet other instances, particular hegemonic groups, ranging from representatives of the nation state to national elites as well as the leaders of orthodox religious movements, may appropriate either cultural forms or performances associated with minority groups in attempts to legitimate their own rule.

Televisual as well as cinematic forms of representation are often thought to be conduits for as well as products of modernity. These products are seen to be part of a broader range of cosmopolitan cultural practices, such as fashion, sport, tourism, restaurant-going and museum attendance, in which much of the world's population presently participates. But modernity is an uneven process, not a uniform one. Rofel has proposed that rather than regarding modernity as 'a specific set of practices', it is best apprehended 'as an ideological trope – both in Europe and elsewhere. As such, it generates meaningful struggles because people have a commitment to the term' (1997: 160). She argues that 'modernity is a story that people tell themselves about themselves in relation "to others". It is a powerful story because nation-states organize the body politic around it' (Rofel 1997; Dirks 1990).

Many of the chapters in this volume examine diverse forms of media representation ranging from commercial and/or state media documentation, to indigenous cultural productions, to viewings of Hollywood soap operas, which now form part of diverse performative or ritual events both in non-western and western settings. The chapters reveal the divergent effects of media involvement as well as the unpredictable meanings which local viewers assign to media products (Crain 1997; Hahn 1994). Similar to the argument that there are alternative paths to modernity distinct from the monolithic Euro-American experience, these analyses suggest that there is no uniform experience of the media. Rather than presupposing *a priori* that engagement with media products has a homogenising effect, and thereby replaces either 'local identities, localized forms of meaning' (Peters 1997: 86), or 'local activities' (Hughes-Freeland, this volume), many of our contributors demonstrate that only detailed empirical investigations undertaken at the micro level can provide evidence which either affirms or negates this presumption.

While the ruling blocs of many nation states draw on media forms to communicate messages to their citizenries regarding national development and religious conduct, they are also preoccupied by their inability to regulate the inflow of transnational messages, in the form of pirate films or cassettes as well as foreign television broadcasts which have been smuggled across their borders or penetrated their airwaves (Hughes-Freeland, this volume). Transnational media products have a potential levelling effect. Providing local viewers with access to 'global time' (Wilk 1994), the messages and imagery they convey may delegit-imise the official discourses of respective nation states.

Although MacAloon has suggested that ritual, drama and so forth can be included in the category of 'spectacle' (1984), there is a strong case for the claim that ritual cannot be subsumed or reproduced through media representations (Hughes-Freeland 1998). As Caldarola has argued, 'change is increasingly the product of altered representa-tions' (1994: 66), and, as he continues,

> the simulacra of mass media are as much simulations as any of the more pedestrian forms of representation encoded in ritual activity, the arts, performance and narrative traditions, and so we should not be surprised if anthropological analyses of mass media resemble studies of these more conventional forms.
>
> (Caldarola 1994: 68)

There is, however, an important difference between ritual and the experience of events mediated by television or print. Unlike a ritual event in a shared physical space, the media event is decontextualised, disconnected, diffused, re-used. However, recent studies based on ethnographic research have proposed connections, rather than contrasts, between events mediated by technology and those attended in a specific time and place. Little (1995) has explored the dislocation and relocation by the media of the Rio Earth Summit to challenge and redeploy anthropological perspectives on ritual. Arguments about the engagement of the self with media also support different presupposi-tions about identity and its transformations. Pink (1998) discusses how a viewer changes identities, breaking the narrative of one role to switch to another. Instead of having fixed identities, the television viewer is constituted by variable agency (see Griffin 1996). Engagement with events in their media versions makes possible a less atomistic analysis of the social actor, revealing a person's social roles as multiplex, contin-gent and flexible. Comparative ethnographic analysis of media and ritual practices can also demonstrate a refutation of any universal notions of the constitution of the self. Hirsch (1998) argues that culturally based forms of identity construction are demonstrated in particular local instances of media and ritual practice. In contrast to Pink, he argues that ethnographies of television viewing in the West may under some circumstances demonstrate an atomisation of the self, but in Papua New Guinea, where identity resides in ritual exchange, practices reveal different forms of local identity predicated on different cultural ideas of selfhood. Rather than locating media and ritual in a neo-evolutionist perspective, Hirsch argues that particular practices reveal particular forms of local identity which are based on cultural ideas of selfhood. This argument has also been made about responses to television viewing in Tonga (Hahn 1994) and Papua (Willson and Kuhlick 1994).

Anthropologists have already established procedures which will usefully further the exploration of the relationship between forms of life which may be non-quotidian or mundane, real or contrived, tangible or vicarious; forms of life which have been the subject of ritual analysis, and which are also part of how we understand the role of media in social life. Despite their claims to deconstruct, many post-modern accounts from media or performance studies maintain the (modernist and occidentalist) Cartesian view of the relationship between human nature and social action – albeit in a new version of 'I consume therefore I am'. This assumption alone should make the anthropologist chary of allowing consumption to consume ritual.

Either explicitly or implicitly, the chapters in this volume bring a performative perspective to recent concerns with consumption. The performative model has been available to social analysts for the last fifty years, and although criticised for carrying overly western perspectives on action and truth (Schieffelin 1998), it is nonetheless a useful counter to the more recent model of social action as expressed through the metaphor of consumption. Consumption itself is not immune from criticism, as anthropology's latest act of ethnocentrism (Hobart n.d.). In particular, the performative and creative aspects of human behaviour restore to the notion of identity the agentive dimension which is underplayed in cultural models of identity.[1] Wagner's (1981) conception of culture as doubly inventive offers one illustration of creative generation. He focuses on forms of indigenous inventive creativity which are subsequently reinvented within anthropological frames of representation. A generative model of identity permits a dialectical engagement of the personal and the collective which is underplayed in the cultural model that emphasised collective determinants. It also suggests that identity might require a connection with doing rather than being. In these terms, identity is interactive, and is based on activities which occur in specific situations, and the way these resonate across time and space, through words spoken in transient gossip and inscribed in lasting stories and scripts.

In this volume, then, the performative model captures themes of ritual, media and identity, but at same time some approaches to 'consumption' give readers, consumers, individuals and collective groups a great deal of agency, as regards refashioning products purchased in the market place. In contrast to the cultural studies approach, anthropological authors describe consumption practices from the point of view of agents (Howes 1996) or what Lavie and Swedenburg (1996) have called 'lived experience'. Society is thus driven by people who are active viewers of television programmes, who read *Rambo*, *Dallas*, etc., according to their own cultural or subcultural codes (Crain, Bovin, Hughes-Freeland, this volume).

Exploring themes: intersections and points of departure

Our six case studies focus on ritual and identity. Several of them explore ritual and identities in relation to the media (Crain, Hughes-Freeland) while others pay more attention to identity and the performative aspects of ritual (Bovin, Hoëm, Mitchell, Rudie). The chapters present us with different ways of thinking about identity which emerge from the conjunction of ritual and/or performance. The processual understanding of 'ritualisation' and 'performativity' illuminates the processual aspect of identity-making, in opposition to the conceptualisation of identities as essential, fixed or homogeneous. The chapters examine the ways in which diverse identities are created within specific contexts while also drawing attention to subtle shifts or transformations of these identities as they are negotiated, affirmed or contested over the course of time. Notions of collective identity elaborated in performative contexts entail different forms of self-expression or self-definition which distinguish particular 'selves' from 'others', and most chapters in this volume break with the one-to-one correspondence between 'identity' and 'habitus' that Langman discusses (1992), by focusing on particular contexts in which groups essentialise their identities.[2]

The theme of multiple identities is examined in a number of ways. Hoëm's chapter demonstrates that new identities cannot be imposed *ad hoc* or be readily exchanged. A theatre group of Tokelauans who have lived in New Zealand reconfigure elements of a traditional clown skit to create a play intended to provoke critical reflections of traditional behaviour within the atoll community that would ultimately bring about social change. The play juxtaposes notions of selfhood based on a communal, kin-oriented ethic with a modern New Zealand-style ethic based on individual choice. Contrary to the actor's intentions, during the rehearsals in New Zealand and performances in Tokelau, many individual actors came to realise that the mode of self-hood they could play in New Zealand was 'unplayable' in Tokelau. Hoëm shows how notions of selfhood as well as the meanings of particular performances are defined and acquired within specific contexts/places. Rudie also raises questions about the extent to which symbols or images of the female athlete are exchangeable across cultures in the global meeting place of Olympic sport. Rudie is concerned with the audience – specifically the Norwegian audience – but other chapters tackle the challenge to cultural homogeneity not only at the level of performance, but also in the response to perfor-mances. Hoëm breaks down individual responses both of the atoll audience and of the theatre troupe, and does not speak of identity in a collectivist way. Hughes-Freeland also juxtaposes stereotypic represen-tations of Balineseness with specific contexts which test the limits of homogenised culture concepts. She argues that Balinese people perform to external expectations of Balineseness, but that they do so according to their personal histories and personalities. Crain also explores how identities of elites and *indígenas* in Ecuador are contra-dictory and often shift as a result of contextual cues. Both groups mobilise diverse self-images during performance at the feast of San Juan in order to make political statements to others. These so called 'local identities' of both *indígenas* and elites are global constructions. Like the WoDaaBe nomads dwelling in the Sahel (Bovin, this volume), the *indígenas* risk essentialising their identity as a provisional political strategy in their confrontations with others (see Lavie and Swedenburg 1996).

A number of chapters focus on the gendered aspects of social iden-tity (Rudie, Mitchell, Bovin). Rudie examines the performance of femininity in the context of the 1994 Winter Olympic Games in Lillehammer, Norway. She demonstrates that there is a movement towards gender equality in the performance of cross-country skiing, but that figure skating reinforces gender hierarchies. The contradictory gender scripts encountered in the diverse disciplines of contemporary sport are evidence that gender identities are neither fixed nor homoge-neous. Rudie concentrates on the local Norwegian interpretations of these sports, but leaves us with several questions to consider: Is global ritual an unmanageable concept? Do the physical demands of sporting performance constrain human creativity in such a way as to favour a view of gender as fixed by laws of nature, and not as something which is socially constructed?

Whereas Rudie's analysis of the performance of gender identities concentrates on femininities, Mitchell explores the construction of masculinities in everyday life and the performance of Catholic rituals in Malta. In his analysis, there is no single monolithic masculinity, and even hegemonic masculinity is performed in different ways, producing different variants. Carrying the heavy statues produces large calluses on the men's bodies that signify hegemonic masculinity and also trustworthiness, being a good father. They also affirm heterosexuality in relation to the successful performances of feminine gender identities associated both with women's kin work in the public sphere as well as their exclusive control over everyday activities in the domestic sphere. The process also defines others categories of masculinity (homosexuals and 'fuckers'). Bovin's chapter also explores masculinity, but in the context of intercultural construction. To western outsiders, the performative displays by WoDaaBe men of the African Sahel contradict stereotypes of male self-presentation, and as a result, these dances have attracted media attention. Magazines such as *Elle* and the *National Geographic*, as well as the audience at London's National Film Theatre construct WoDaaBe identities as 'exotic nomads'. The author argues that the WoDaaBe are increasingly aware both of the presence of spectators during their diverse performances as well as the far-reaching impact of media representations. Films and magazine articles focus on the painted male faces, which become a sign of the exotic other. In response to outside interest and local pressures on their survival as a group, the WoDaaBe have deliberately internalised this essential exoticism in order to strengthen the boundaries of their own cultural identity in a region well known for its social structural complexity and environmental difficulties.

Social performance produces variable forms of social identity which connect with different levels of community and collectivity. Thus Mitchell shows how the ritual of *San Pawl* simultaneously asserts Catholic hegemony while also reproducing national identity. Crain also examines Catholic ritual, in this case the patron saint festival of *San Juan*, a former patron-client ritual in highland Ecuador. This has been redirected towards 'performative ends', becoming an arena in which members of a cosmopolitan elite family and *indígenas* engage in identity politics. These identities are the product both of the rural hacienda context and of a particular historical conjuncture, in which this elite family traffics in a transnational sign-economy, and *indígenas* have gained access to new sources of power (alliances and coalitions with groups) both inside and outside Ecuador, which have helped them to bypass controls which elites could formerly impose upon them.

The effects of media might be expected to further complicate this process of multiple levels of identity and engagement, as demonstrated in the chapters by Hughes-Freeland and Bovin. Rather than producing cultural homogeneity, the media can produce local effects and responses. Hughes-Freeland describes how in Bali, people watched a live and a broadcast version of the same play, and contrary to expectation, considered the televised version better able to express Balinese artistry in the context of preserving the traditional image of Balinese culture within the Indonesian nation state. As mediated by television, the *arja* plays did not exclude the active agency of the viewers, but rather affirmed the men's local identities as Balinese individuals who are also Indonesian citizens. In Bovin's example, the WoDaaBe perform masculinity against the state – as a conscious intensification of their 'exoticness' and their foregrounding of their cultural difference. It is a political act, necessary to attract international attention to their plight and secure their survival. Outside interest becomes a way of reinforcing local interest. Whereas in Bali watching television can serve as a rite of affirmation of personal identity and knowledge, the WoDaaBe respond to external media interest in them to firm up their own ethnic identities by projecting unique images of WoDaaBeness.

Despite the strong evidence for local variation, none of the contributors is convinced that locality and patterns of choice will necessarily remain congruent. In Bali recent deregulation has given audiences more choice of what to watch, and viewers are choosing to watch Hollywood films instead of state-sponsored programmes aimed at developing and preserving the national heritage. Likewise, Rudie seems to imply that as the Winter Olympics has become a worldwide media event, particular kinds of femininity are vested in biological rather than cultural categories. As culture becomes diasporic, the category of nature may become re-essentialised on a global stage. Similarly, in Mitchell's analysis of Malta lurks a question about the degree to which the media's presence reinforces hegemonic linkages between local *festa* performances of *San Pawl* in which a specific form of masculinity is produced in accordance with the goals of nation-building.

These arguments indicate that state control of media regulates identity, including gendered identity. However, the chapters do not suggest that state competence is as powerful as embodied presence. Bovin, Hughes-Freeland, Mitchell and Rudie all argue in their different ways for the power of embodied presence and the importance of skill over and above the effectiveness of top-down control and collectivisation. Both Crain and Bovin note how global media reframe ritual performance as a media attraction, and they also make a strong case for performance being a scene in which identities are enacted. Crain adds another dimension to her analysis, and includes an examination of the historical role of elites in attracting media. For her, the situation is not so much local versus global, or local versus the centre, but the articulation of power across communities, in an arena of negotiation in which the stakes are loaded: people have choice, but some have more power to choose and better access to the means of communication than others.

The chapters

Ingjerd Hoëm focuses on performance of a play by a group of Tokelauans. These Tokelauans are members of an emigrant community in New Zealand, and have refashioned a theatrical form traditionally recognised as a humorous event by residents of the tiny atoll, to project alternative images of selfhood which challenge traits typically associated with 'the Tokelauan way'. Hoëm explores the mixed responses to the play, in which moral attributes such as individualistic choice prevail over a more communalistic orientation. She also foregrounds issues of reflexivity by attending to relations between the performers' desired intentions and the play's reception by local audiences. Efforts to critique 'the Tokelauan way', by replacing it with an alternative model of selfhood, did not convey the same message either to Tokelauan New Zealanders or to local Tokelauans when performed on the native atoll. Unexpected and occasionally negative responses during rehearsals in New Zealand and to the performance in Tokelau made the actors aware that notions of selfhood are tied to place and context. These factors influence which notion of selfhood will prevail.

Felicia Hughes-Freeland's chapter also explores questions of identity in relation to the specific performance of particular plays. Her analysis is based on indigenous responses to the contexts of performance, and draws on ethnographic material from a long-term project on cultural transformation in Bali, Indonesia. Television broadcasting has been available in Bali since 1977. Using taped television programmes and video recordings of live performances, this paper presents preliminary findings, and concentrates on a comparison of one *arja* play in two different performance contexts, one ritual, one broadcast, through the comments of a small Balinese audience. She asks

about the way in which 'Bali' and 'Balinese culture' have been represented in a number of contexts, including the anthropological one, and
argues that Bali, long seen by outsiders as quintessentially exotic,
should be analysed in a modern context. Modernity, however, is not
uniform. The indigenous commentaries presented in this chapter challenge the researcher's categories, and suggest alternative orders of
difference. These ethnographic findings indicate that watching television can act as a rite of affirmation of identity which is transformative
and polyvalent, inflected according to specific situations. It is also
important to consider long-term structural processes, and to note that
in understanding local appropriation of global technologies, the
conscious reasoning of local subjects is itself the result of structuring
factors.

Jon Mitchell's analysis of ritual performance in Malta demonstrates
how a particular type of hegemonic masculinity is produced. The
chapter focuses on statue-carrying in the feast (*festa*) of St Paul, the
national patron saint and also the local patron saint in the parish where
research was conducted. Statue-carrying produces a particular category
of heterosexual men, the *reffiegha*, who gain a status both local and
national. This status is inscribed on the very body of these men in the
form of a large callus on the shoulder, which serves as a focus for and a
sign of their performative competence. Whereas other theorists have
studied the ritual production of gender identity in one-off events associated with initiation, this chapter proposes a dialectical relationship
between the spectacular ritual performance of statue-carrying and the
everyday activities associated with masculinity in Malta. The identities
in question are produced between performance as event and the
performativity of everyday actions. The performance occurs on a
national stage produced through broadcast television and the circula-
tion of video footage. This ensures that the *festa* is significant both at
the personal level for the statue-carriers and at the public level for local
and national ritual constituencies.

Mette Bovin offers an African example of the significance of dance
performance for the production of masculine and ethnic identity. In
the eyes of the European media, the WoDaaBe are the most 'exotic' of
the Fulani group, and indeed they themselves practise 'active archaisation' – a constant reinvention and intensification of tradition. The
WoDaaBe have increasingly essentialised their identities to match
western stereotypes of them as independent and culturally distinct
nomads who are isolated from the influences of modernity. The author
argues that by conforming to dominant image-making, the WoDaaBe

attract the attention of western audiences necessary for their survival in the drought-ridden Sahel. Such performances include annual male beauty contests in which 'Mr WoDaaBe' is selected by a jury of three young women from a clan which competes with that of the performers. The pronounced male vanity and use of cosmetics and mirrors by young men is unique to WoDaaBe. It is a central way in which they define their identity as WoDaaBe, within the sub-group of the Fulani, and *vis-à-vis* the sedentarising pressures from the nation states around which they journey.

The construction of gendered identity, this time female, is the theme of Ingrid Rudie's chapter, which contributes to an emergent literature on performance and the anthropology of public events by drawing on research at the Winter Olympic Games at Lillehammer, Norway, in 1994. The athlete is a key symbol, and Rudie makes a historical comparison of female athletes in international cross-country skiing and figure skating competitions to analyse two issues: the relation between sport and changing societal discourses regarding gender; and the degree to which meanings can be shared across cultures. The two sports portray two distinct symbolic universes: cross-country skiing since the 1950s has been characterised by a movement towards gender equality; however, in figure skating, notions about female glamour and youthfulness continue to prevail, making it difficult to compare male and female performances. On one level, these games promote universality and global homogenisation, with their focus on bodily activities, which facilitates communication across cultural, class, age and sexual boundaries. However, on another level, particular sport disciplines have developed within the context of specific local traditions, such that a sport often carries a rich load of tacit social memory. The symbols attached to this memory are not easily translatable, and may foster a sense of cultural fragmentation. Rudie demonstrates the complexity and contradictory messages regarding gendered scripts encountered in the arena of international sport, in which the principles of gender hierarchy coexist alongside those of gender equality.

Turning from participation in sporting performance to participation in ritual performance, Mary M. Crain asks what it means to be a member of a 'local ritual' community in a global era. Ethnographic analysis of *San Juan*, a patron saint celebration which momentarily draws together cosmopolitan elites and globally savvy *indígenas* ('indigenous people') in the community of Quimsa, in the Ecuadorean Andes, illuminates the changing cultural landscape characterising everyday life in the late twentieth century. Recognised regionally as the

'Indian saint' *par excellence*, it is composed of a sequence of performances which speak to a range of publics. During the first sequence,
the elites are excluded from participation, and performances of music
and dance traditions occur among *indígenas*. The latter have incorporated imported media technology such as VCRs and tape recorders as
elements of this celebration, and in many instances such technology
has revitalised this tradition. On the third day, the climax of *San Juan*,
the cosmopolitan elites, as well as development agents, foreign ambas-
sadors and tourists, journey to Quimsa for the occasion. It is argued
that contemporary *San Juan* is best comprehended not as a nostalgic
effort to revitalise a formerly harmonious, albeit hierarchical ritual, but
as a contested arena, in which both cosmopolitan elites and *indígenas*
engage in globally informed performances of their identity politics.

Future directions

The range of events and regions discussed bring together cultural
production and cultural reproduction to argue that identity must not
be understood as monolithic and essential. Forms of identity which
bring together the personal and the social are interactive and situa-
tional. Identity is polythetic, but it is not infinite; gender, for example,
sets different kinds of limits on social actors. The contributors variously
explore the scope and limits of identity production within the sphere of
ritual performance, and test the hypothesis that such performance is
only socially effective if it carries a sense of truth. This in turn allows a
theoretical exploration of the relationship between social reality, imagination and its products, power, and fantasy as they contribute to
human survival.

The evidence presented here gives hope for humanism winning out
against fears that future forms of being and knowing will be deter-
mined by structures of global technology which infuse our
consciousness and constrain our agency to the point that we become
'cultural dopes' (Giddens 1979, criticising Parsons), or even 'techno
dopes'. The evidence of this volume indicates that consumption is too
narrow a term to express the core of social action, and suggests that a
performative model has wider analytical significance. The way in which
identity is understood has always summed up the world view of an era
or region. For a long time rationality lay at the heart of the western
sense of person and being. The cultural relativism of anthropology
challenged that model, and recently there has been a paradigm shake-
up, if not a clear shift, in which there have been pleas to restore the

body to identity. While both performance and consumption models are invoked in these debates, there is a danger that identity and representation are becoming conflated with one another. It would seem that anthropologists might pause and consider identity less as being, and more in terms of doing, and think in terms of social reproduction, rather than simply cultural production. This emphasis would take us back to the basic concerns with social action and behaviour, with inter-action, roles, relations and constraints. Such traditional concerns of course are always with us, but they require fresh modelling, to tackle the perennial problem of dichotomising the relationship of the macro to the micro, a relationship which becomes increasingly salient as tech-nology expands.

This volume argues for the value of the fine-grained studies resulting from ethnographic research and the insights this provides for resituating our analyses of 'ritualisation' to fit the coordinates of an increasingly interconnected world. Interconnections of a disciplinary nature have also concerned us while editing this book, and we have debated in particular what the relationship between anthropology and cultural and media studies should be.

Within anthropology, ethnographers engage in dialogues over lengthy periods of time both with individuals and groups in different parts of the world. Cultural (and media) studies have a different conceptual order, and interpret/decode cultural texts such as films, novels, drama, popular music and soap operas, usually from the vantage point of North American or British audiences. Cultural studies pays little attention to the reception of western cultural products beyond the First World, and neither examines what people do with these products nor analyses local interpretive practices.

This book does not sit easily within the corpus of cultural studies, as its chapters analyse performances which engage with, or restyle foreign media which have become 'indigenised', 'creolised' or 'hybridised' in non-Euro-American settings. Appadurai (1996: 52) in particular has highlighted the need to think further about how contemporary identi-ties are produced by reciprocal interaction between both individual and collective fantasies and 'mediascapes' which offer a wide range of scenarios for 'possible lives'. His outline of a 'cosmopolitan ethnog-raphy' is articulated primarily at the macro level, or works intertextually from Latin American literary sources. Appadurai moves cross-culturally in a manner which cultural studies has not, but although his analysis is theoretically stimulating, it ultimately endorses much of the logic informing cultural studies. By privileging 'texts', cultural studies fails to take into account that everyday lived experience is not simply a coherent script which can be 'read', critiqued. Hirsch (1998) has made a strong case for the power of anthropological ethnography in contrast to what is considered ethnography in media studies. Paul Willis, one of the few people working in cultural studies to 'do' ethnography in a manner recognisable to anthropologists, has also noted how cultural and media studies neglect the struggles of daily life which lie behind the texts, and produce rather predictable findings:

> There is a desperate need within the theoreticised cultural studies for a theoretically informed fieldwork practice which allows for 'surprise', and which gives scope for thick description to produce data not prefigured in theoretical starting-positions.
>
> (Willis, in Wade 1997: 41)[3]

There are ethnocentric assumptions implicit in the paradigms of cultural studies. Anthropological knowledge by contrast is based on ethnographic findings which are produced intersubjectively in particular localities which refract global processes through the optic of local imaginations. Analyses wrought from culture studies proceed from very different epistemological foundations, and pursue other objectives.

We both agree that anthropology has a distinctive voice which it should retain. The validity of Appadurai's pronouncements needs to be tested further through global as well as theoretically informed ethnographic work on the interconnections between identity, media, creativity and performance undertaken at the micro level. Beyond this, we would endorse Caldarola's plea (1994: 67) that we reconceptualise thematic areas currently defined restrictively as 'visual anthropology' by expanding this field of knowledge to include 'an anthropology of the visual', a process already well in train (Banks and Morphy 1997). Similarly, as has been argued, interconnections between disciplines can help to develop an 'anthropology of the imaginary' as well as an ethnographic analysis of the ways in which specific iconographies constitute diverse social worlds (Hughes-Freeland 1998: 23). This resonates with comments voiced by diverse authors (Appadurai 1996; Taussig 1993), who are concerned respectively with 'the increasing importance of the imagination in contemporary social life' as well as with the power of the image to motivate individuals and social groups to express desires, both past and present (Kane 1994). Such insights are being developed within anthropology with reference to insights from cultural studies, performance studies and critical theory (Appadurai 1996; Buck-Morris 1989; Castoriadas 1987; Coombe 1997; Freedburg 1989; Lavie and Swedenburg 1996; Minh-ha 1989; Rosaldo 1989).

In conclusion, it is a sign of anthropology's resilience and contemporary relevance that the disciplinary disagreements and debates referred to above are being aired directly. We would both hope to see the continuing emergence of fruitful contradictions which generate further enquiries and further understandings.

Notes

1 A recent cultural studies text models the 'the circuit of culture' as 'flows' between identity and production and consumption, and between representation and regulation; the circuit is completed by a link between consumption and regulation (Du Gay *et al.* 1997: 3). While it could be argued that production operates as action in this model, it results in consumption, and identity as a concept (collective and personal or individual) is thus defined through production and consumption, rather than through performance and the creative generation of identity.

2 Langman outlines an approach compatible with the analyses pursued in many of the following case studies:

> The public expressions and presentations of socialized selfhood, the persona, are supposed to be the surface manifestations of an underlying unified core of the person. But with the influence of so many models in diverse realities, and the unending bombardment of media images, it seems more likely that identity is expressed in a variety of provisional identities, or self-images, that may serve as templates or strategies for self-presentations in *specific* situations. While the person has a more or less stable temperament, memories of selfhood across various times and activities, and has learned and internalized the socially constructed *habitus* of their society which includes a notion of selfhood, the trans-situational stability of identity may be more imputed than real.
>
> (1992: 57; also Crain 1996)

3 Willis, paradoxically, was seconding the motion 'Cultural studies will be the death of anthropology', a motion which, not surprisingly perhaps, was defeated, with nineteen votes in favour, thirty-four against, twelve abstentions and two spoiled papers (Wade 1997: 71).

Bibliography

Anderson, B. (1983) *Reflections on the Origin and Spread of Nationalism*, London: Verso.

Appadurai, A. (1996) *Modernity at Large: Cultural Dimensions of Globalization*, Minneapolis MN: University of Minnesota Press.

Banks, M. and Morphy, H. (1997) Introduction to *Rethinking Visual Anthropology*, New Haven CT: Yale University Press.

Bell, C. (1992) *Ritual Theory, Ritual Practice*, Oxford: Oxford University Press.

Buck-Morris, S. (1989) *The Dialectics of Seeing: Walter Benjamin and the Arcades Project*, Cambridge MA: MIT Press.

Caldarola, V. (1994) 'Embracing the Media Simulacrum', *Visual Anthropology Review*, 10, 1: 66–9.

Castoriadas, C. (1987) [1975] *The Imaginary Institution of Society*, Cambridge MA: MIT Press.

Coleman, S. and Elsner, J. (1998) 'Performing Pilgrimage: Walsingham and the Ritual Construction of Irony', in F. Hughes-Freeland (ed.) *Ritual, Performance, Media*, London and New York: Routledge.

Coombe, R. (1997) 'The Demonic Place of the "Not There": Trademark Rumours in the Postindustrial Imaginary', in A. Gupta and J. Ferguson (eds) *Culture, Power, Place: Explorations in a Critical Anthropology*, Durham NC: Duke University Press.

Crain, M. M. (1996) 'The Gendering of Ethnicity in the Ecuadorean Highlands: Native Women's Self-fashioning in the Urban Marketplace', in M. Melhuus and K. A. Stølen (eds) *Machos, Mistresses and Madonnas: Contesting the Power of Latin American Gender Imagery*, London: Verso.

——(1997) 'The Remaking of an Andalusian Pilgrimage Tradition: Debates Regarding Visual (Re)presentations and the Meaning of "Locality" in a Global Era', in A. Gupta and J. Ferguson (eds) *Culture, Power, Place: Explorations in a Critical Anthropology*, Durham NC: Duke University Press.

Dirks, N. (1990) 'History as a Sign of the Modern', *Public Culture*, 2, 2: 25–32.

Du Gay, P., Hall, S., Janes, L., Mackay, H. and Negus, K. (1997) *Doing Cultural Studies: The Story of the Sony Walkman*, London: Sage.

Freedburg, D. (1989) *The Power of Images: Studies in the History and Theory of Response*, Chicago IL: University of Chicago Press.

Geertz, C. (1973) *The Interpretation of Cultures*, New York: Basic Books.

Gerholm, T. (1988) 'On Ritual: a Postmodern View', *Ethnos*, 3, 4: 190–203.

Giddens, A. (1979) *Central Problems in Social Theory: Action, Structure and Contradiction in Social Analysis*, London: Macmillan.

Griffin, C. (1996) 'Experiencing Power: Dimensions of Gender, "Race" and Class', in N. Charles and F. Hughes-Freeland (eds) *Practising Feminism: Identity, Difference, Power*, London: Routledge.

Gross, J., MacMurray, D. and Swedenburg, T. (1994) 'Arab Noise and Ramadan Nights: Rai, Rap and Franco-Maghreb Identity', *Diaspora*, 3, 1: 3–40.

Hahn, E. (1994) 'The Tongan Tradition of Going to the Movies', *Visual Anthropology Review*, 10, 1: 103–11.

Hannerz, U. (1989) 'Notes on the Global Ecumene', *Public Culture*, 1, 2: 66–75.

Hirsch, E. (1998) 'Bound and Unbound Entities: Reflections on the Ethnographic Perspectives of Anthropology vis-à-vis Media and Cultural Studies', in F. Hughes-Freeland (ed.) *Ritual, Performance, Media* (ASA monograph 35), London and New York: Routledge.

Hobart, M. (n.d.) 'Consuming Passions: Overinterpreting Television-viewing in Bali', paper presented to the ASA conference *Ritual, Performance, Media*, Swansea, March 1996.

Howes, D. (ed.) (1996) *Cross-Cultural Consumption: Global Markets, Local Realities*, London: Routledge.

Hughes-Freeland, F. (ed.) (1998) Introduction to *Ritual, Performance, Media* (ASA monograph 35), London and New York: Routledge.

Langman, L. (1992) 'Neon Cages: Shopping for Subjectivity', in R. Shields (ed.) *Lifestyle Shopping: The Subject of Consumption*, London: Routledge.

Lavie, S. and Swedenburg, T. (eds) (1996) Introduction to *Displacement, Diaspora and Geographies of Identity*, Durham NC: Duke University Press.

Little, P. E. (1995) 'Ritual, Power and Ethnography at the Rio Earth Summit', *Critique of Anthropology*, 15, 3: 265–88.

MacAloon, J. (ed.) (1984) Introduction to *Rite, Drama, Festival, Spectacle: Rehearsals Towards a Theory of Performance*, Philadelphia PA: Institute for the Study of Human Issues.

Parkin, D. (1992) 'Ritual as Spatial Direction and Bodily Division', in D. de Coppet (ed.) *Understanding Rituals*, London and New York: Routledge.

Peters, J. D. (1997) 'Seeing Bifocally: Media, Place, Culture', in A. Gupta and J. Ferguson (eds) *Culture, Power, Place: Explorations in Critical Anthropology*, Durham NC: Duke University Press.

Pink, S. (1998) 'From Ritual Sacrifice to Media Commodity: Anthropological and Media Constructions of the Spanish Bullfight and the Rise of Women Performers', in F. Hughes-Freeland (ed.) *Ritual, Performance, Media* (ASA monograph 35), London and New York: Routledge.

Rofel, L. (1997) 'Rethinking Modernity: Space and Factory Discipline in China', in A. Gupta and J. Ferguson (eds) *Culture, Power, Place: Explorations in Critical Anthropology*, Durham NC: Duke University Press.

Rosaldo, R. (1989) *Culture and Truth: The Remaking of Social Analysis*, Boston MA: Beacon Press.

Schieffelin, E. L. (1998) 'Problematizing Performance', in F. Hughes-Freeland (ed.) *Ritual, Performance, Media* (ASA monograph 35), London and New York: Routledge.

Taussig, M. (1993) *Mimesis and Alterity: A Particular History of the Senses*, New York and London: Routledge.

——(1997) *The Magic of the State*, London: Routledge.

Trinh, T. Minh-ha (1989) *Woman, Native, Other: Writing Postcoloniality and Feminism*, Bloomington IN: Indiana University Press.

Turner, V. (1969) *The Ritual Process: Structure and Anti-Structure*, Ithaca NY: Cornell University Press.

Wade, P. (ed.) (1997) *Cultural Studies will be the Death of Anthropology: Mark Hobart and Paul Willis vs Nigel Rapport and John Gledhill*, The GDAT Debate no. 8, Manchester: Group for Debates in Anthropological Theory.

Wagner, R. (1981) *The Invention of Culture*, Chicago IL: Chicago University Press.

Wilk, R. R. (1994) 'Colonial Time and TV Time: Television and Temporality in Belize', *Visual Anthropology Review*, 10, 1: 94–102.

Willson, M. and Kulick, D. (1994) 'Rambo's Wife Saves the Day: Subjugating the Gaze and Subverting the Narrative in a Papua New Guinean Swamp', *Visual Anthropology Review* 10, 2: 1–13.

Chapter 2

Clowns, dignity and desire

On the relationship between performance, identity and reflexivity

Ingjerd Hoëm

Introduction

'Every chief needs a clown', Vilsoni Hereniko (1994) states rhetorically in a debate about clowning seen as social criticism. Hereniko presents a broad analysis of the relationship between institutionalised power, represented in South Pacific societies by positions such as kings, chiefs, priests and elders, and the subversive power that lies in humorous performances. The Polynesian clowns' licence to subvert has tradition-ally been granted due to the clowns' close association with potentially malevolent spirits. Hereniko proposes that clowning activities in Pacific societies generally can be seen as a kind of remedy that serves to coun-teract the tendency for people in positions of authority to become cut off from the voices of the grassroots. Even if one chooses to disregard the more obvious functionalist implications of Hereniko's argument, it would seem reasonable to assume that the relationship between people acting in 'king-like' capacities and people acting, more or less volun-tarily, as 'clowns', can be a highly ambiguous one. But before entering into an empirically based discussion of this kind of relationship, I shall outline a theoretical approach for examining relations between perfor-mances, selfhood and reflexivity.

The existential aspects of identity formation

For the purposes of this article I shall employ a definition of 'perfor-mance' that focuses on playful, theatrical action (Schieffelin 1985; Kapferer 1986; Turner 1987). The performative genres that I shall discuss, namely clowning, skit making and action theatre, occur within a larger context of Tokelau festive gatherings called *fiafia* ('to be happy', 'happiness'). These contexts are clearly set apart from the ordinary routine of everyday life, and are characterised by a marked degree of ritualisation, thus creating a pattern which is identifiable in all such events. Some of these elements represent historical continuities with pre-contact, pre-Christian Tokelau, others are more recent innovations. However, contemporary gatherings are conceptualised more as feasts than as religious events. Tokelau, like many other societies in the Pacific, is known for its 'performative cast', that is, interaction in general is oriented towards what Goffman (1959) has described as 'face work'. This factor creates a continuity between everyday life and the festive occasions, in that the morality associated with 'face' and which permeates everyday interaction, is made the object of discussion, criticism, hilarity and ridicule, through skits and clowning which are important ingredients in the festive gatherings (Hoëm 1995).

My main argument is that, in the anthropological study of performance, we should seek to include the perspectives of individual actors to a greater extent than is frequently the case. I do not for instance share Maurice Bloch's somewhat pessimistic view that the attempt to grasp what rituals or other social events 'mean to the participants and onlookers' is ultimately an impossible task (Bloch 1986: 11).

Bloch's statement must be examined in the light of his broader argument that the study of cognitive aspects of cultural production must be grounded in sociological studies. I have argued the merits of this approach elsewhere, and I do not have any quarrel with this premise (Hoëm 1995). However, I shall maintain that it is of great importance for the study of performative events to seek to include the thoughts, dreams and desires of the people who are involved in the production of such events.

Generally, we have seen a move away from analyses of the form and structure of the performance as an object of study in its own right, towards a greater inclusion of processes of production. In addition to the focus on the relationship between the ritual or performative event and everyday life, this insistence on taking the processes of production into account has also led to a greater awareness of the experiential depth we may gain by including the perspectives of the people involved.[1]

This approach opens the possibility of an explicit integration of peoples' reflexive capacities into the study of the actual interaction that produces cultural events such as those that we frequently describe as performances. In other words, this approach represents a counter-argument to the general assumption permeating even more recent anthropological works, that reflexivity be seen as a practice associated only with people whose lives are circumscribed by a modernity closely associated with the canons of western forms of literacy.[2]

Taking what Geertz (1983) has called the 'native point of view' into account in the broad manner that I have just briefly outlined, implies lending particular attention to the question of how performative events are conceptualised. This approach leads us to explore what kind of social spaces performative events are, both in terms of how they are defined locally, but also in more general terms such as the limits and possibilities they set for human agency and thus for the shaping and realisation of identity. In the following, we shall see that a framing of performative events as qualitatively different, namely as matters of importance and as things of no account, has significant implications for how agency is perceived and realised.

My discussion will concentrate on the activities of a Tokelau theatre group. Tokelau is an atoll society which is located in the South Pacific, north of Western Samoa. The members of the theatre group were recruited from the Tokelau community in New Zealand.[3] In this particular case, a confrontation between people who may be said to identify themselves in relation to different models of selfhood, took place within the Tokelau community at large. Furthermore, this confrontation was articulated through the medium of a particular form of performance. I argue that the analysis of this particular form of performance must be carried out by means of a reference to local conceptions of qualitative differences between various social spaces.

My focus on what kind of social space these particular performances provide, and what form of existence they allow people to project, is informed by Friedman's concept of desire as 'a dynamic aspect of the formation of selfhood' (Friedman 1994: 103). I apply this perspective as it throws light on the project of the Tokelau actors themselves and makes it possible to analyse the dilemmas they experienced in a comparative perspective.

Background

Tokelau comprises three atolls, Fakaofo, Nukunonu and Atafu, and is situated in the South Pacific, north of Western Samoa. A fourth atoll, Olohega, is presently US territory, but is claimed by Tokelau as traditionally part of the group. The total number of inhabitants on the atolls is approximately 1,600. Due to alleged overpopulation on the atolls, a New Zealand government-sponsored migration scheme was initiated in the early 1960s. Since that time, people from Tokelau have migrated to New Zealand, and there are now between 4,000 and 5,000 Tokelauans living more or less permanently in New Zealand.[4] Since 1925, Tokelau has been New Zealand territory, but in recent years, and in response to political pressure from the UN towards 'decolonisation', steps have been taken to give Tokelau political independence from New Zealand.

Tension between a communal lifestyle and individualism, brought about by the introduction of a monetary economic sphere, a bureaucracy represented by the Tokelau Public Service (that is, the forces of modernity in general) has been growing in Tokelau at least since the 1960s. The emergence of a generation of Tokelauans who are born in New Zealand, or who have spent time away from the atolls, many of whom have higher-level education, is a more recent phenomenon. Many of the individuals in this group are former scholarship students who have returned to Tokelau for shorter or longer periods, frequently to work in the Tokelau Public Service. This group taken as a whole is highly vocal, and has a common experiential background which differs in significant ways from that of any other group within the Tokelau communities. The main difference lies in the higher degree of exposure of scholarship students to New Zealand society at large, that is, to all socio-economic and institutional levels of the *papalagi* ('European' or 'Caucasian', in Maori terms *pakeha*) culture. Due to their education, they frequently have a wider range of contacts with all levels of New Zealand society, and are not restricted to the lower socio-economic echelons, as is the case with most menial-working, uneducated or unemployed members of the Tokelau communities in New Zealand. This familiarity with *papalagi* society does not, however, in most cases result in a withdrawal from active participation in the Tokelau communities. On the contrary, the trend seems to be that these individuals end up occupying central positions in the Tokelau organisations in New Zealand and within the Tokelau Public Service in Samoa and in Tokelau. They differ from any other group within Tokelau society in the nature of the choices they have had to make to be able to stay in touch with the communities. The activities that I shall describe below were instigated by individuals that represent this segment of Tokelau society.

Humorous performances in Pacific societies

The empirical case that I draw on to illustrate my point is the introduction of action theatre to Tokelau by a group of New Zealand

Tokelauans. This form of theatre is used to further community development, and is commonly used in many Third World countries.

Generally, humorous performances in Pacific societies range from skits to clowning, and cover a broad spectrum from informal to ritual occasions. They all tend to be an integral part of community activity. Although it is the case that much critical commentary is presented through such performances, it is equally the case that in Tokelau conceptions, these performances are not traditionally perceived as instrumental in bringing about changes to the institutional structure of the community. The authority to bring about such changes is traditionally seen as vested in representatives of the formal political structures, such as councils of titled family heads, kings or queens, chiefs or elders.

The difference between the institutionalised power exemplified by a chief or an elder, and the potentially subversive power represented by the clown, is thus also reflected in local conceptualisations of qualitative differences between the social spaces associated with these respective activities.

When discussing various aspects of power in Oceanic societies, it is important to note that scholars seem to agree that what may be called the political and the religious or cosmological aspects of life are very closely associated throughout the region. Thus Hanson (1982), Shore (1982, 1989), Sahlins (1985), Valeri (1985, 1990) and most recently Gell (1995), argue that much ritual behaviour and etiquette permeating everyday life (pre-Christian as well as contemporary) expresses a concern with regulating and controlling the flow of the life-force – in other words what is frequently referred to as *mana*. Dangerous aspects associated with the generative force may adhere to both controlled states (*tapu*) and non-controlled states (*noa*), but in different ways. For example, in Tokelau conceptions, women are still today generally seen as inherently more open to the influence of malevolent and benevolent spirits than men, and as less able to control these forces.[5] Through close association with these spirits, women may become channels of a force that is potentially socially dangerous. It gives them the power as sisters both to heal and destroy, through blessing or cursing their kin. On the other hand, men as family heads may be able to control or regulate such forces by directing them into (and through) political positions or seats (*nofoaga*). This activity is also fraught with dangers in that it is intimately connected with the control of the overall institutional structure of the villages. The clown, in humorous performances, is traditionally granted a temporal licence by ancestral spirits to shake the balance between these institutions – a balance that people go to great lengths to achieve in everyday life.

This concern with regulating the life-force is explicitly expressed in the local discourse concerning the organisation of production and reproduction. A division of extended families (*kaiga*) into two complementary sides serves to channel the flow of goods and produce (Huntsman 1971). This division into complementary sides also serves to control the sexual and procreative relationship between men and women. Individual desires, for sex, for food and so on, are seen as intrinsically anti-social; to act upon such desires for immediate gratification is severely condemned. The person is conceptualised as consisting of this dark, egotistic side, which is complemented by a light, outgoing side. The dark side must be controlled, and the explicit identification of Christianity with the light side seems to have served to emphasise this side at the expense of the side of darkness. The concept that perhaps most clearly reflects the particular form of sociality that takes the form of this smiling, lighthearted, outgoing attitude, is the term *alofa*. This word is frequently translated simply as 'love', but more specifically it denotes sharing, generosity, affection and compassion (Hooper and Huntsman 1996: 115). The high value placed on a collective orientation is also expressed in the concept of *maopoopo* ('to gather together', 'to congregate') with its associations of activities that are well ordered and which involve as many people as possible. This concept expresses a kind of unity between people and what is seen as graceful, harmonious behaviour that they constantly seek to achieve.[6]

As should be apparent from what I have just described, the preoccupation with regulating the generative forces has a very serious quality to it as it concerns matters of life and death, and it produces a particular aesthetic and morality, breaches of which may easily lead to social isolation and in some cases actual death.

The serious nature of this concern permeating the Tokelau way of life is somewhat modified, however, by the importance placed on what is conceptualised as 'things of no account' (*mea tauanoa*). Into this category falls all behaviour that is not of a serious or important nature, that is, unfocused sociality such as walking about aimlessly, idle chatter, and so on. All humorous performances, such as joking, clowning and games, are also examples of such 'things of no account'. An illustration of the considerable value placed on such activities is the fact that in Tokelau in the early 1960s, three consecutive months in the low fishing season around Christmas were set aside each year for games, dancing, clowning and feasting arranged by the two sides (*faitu*) of the village (Hooper 1993).

Humorous performances in Tokelau are defined as *fai mea malie*, 'making sweet or pleasant things', and are an integral part of many occasions, such as games and feasts; they may also occur spontaneously. Skits or *faleaitu*, which means 'house of spirits', depict well-known incidents. These are often drawn from the Bible, but also often parody an event that has happened in Tokelau, frequently caricaturing westerners or Tokelauans trying to act as westerners. An example of an illustration of a skit drawn from the Bible is one made by members of the Women's Committee on Fale, Fakaofo. The scene was about John the Baptist. The old women filled a tub with water and placed it in the middle of the meeting house, where people were gathered, dressed in their best clothes. One of the women, who wore a white angel-costume with wings, proceeded to duck the oldest (and thus highest-ranking) woman present in the tub, and thoroughly drenched her and members of the audience in the process. A skit where the joke was on me was arranged on Nukunonu by a man with a reputation for being a good clown. He had people line up in the middle of the meeting house, and acted as the anthropologist himself. In this capacity he ordered me to 'say some words in my own language', 'to sing a song' and to 'do things the way they are done according to my culture' in front of the village community.

The obvious humorous content of such skits lies in inversion, e.g. by women dressing up and acting as men, ordering people about and so on, or by people who are related as brother and sister acting as if they were a couple (Hooper and Huntsman 1975). In other words, the humorous effect is most frequently achieved by someone acting counter to common morality.[7] In this respect clowns traverse dangerous territory, in that they, in the liminal state provided by the humorous performances, have a licence to subvert the ordinary, everyday balance achieved between what I have described as controlled and uncontrolled states. Thus clowns are truly 'betwixt and between': their activities are neither subject to ordinary restrictions, nor are they completely outside of control – encompassed as their actions are by the safeguarding conceptualisation of this kind of social space as a 'thing of no account'. In other words, the potential danger associated with subversive activities is in the context of this kind of social space modified through the activities being defined as of no account. In contrast, agency in political meetings is conceptualised as of grave importance, and the etiquette which may be subverted by the clown during humorous performances is reinforced with great care within the framework of the political space proper.

However, this local conceptualisation of a qualitative difference between social spaces in terms of how agency is constructed, if taken at face value, has tended to lend itself to structuralist models. That is, it has led to researchers postulating the existence of watertight boundaries between the various social spaces. Thus Shore (1982) contends that clowning activities in Samoa do not affect the political arena proper, in spite of the fact that political issues are frequently explicitly addressed in humorous performances. In Tokelau I have, however, frequently observed a carry-over from humorous performances to political agendas. Admittedly, in most cases this happens in an indirect fashion, that is, through a person in a leadership role being made aware of political opponents' opinions through a humorous performance, and therefore being led to modify a course of action in a subsequent political meeting.

Another way in which humorous performances may affect life outside the performative space is related to the fun in parodying usually being at somebody's expense. Once an incident has been immortalised in a story about 'the time that x did y', through having been turned into a successful skit, it may easily stick to that person's name or reputation, and have a definite and frequently detrimental effect on their standing in the community.

Whereas some individuals are said to have inherited a talent for clowning and thus are active in instigating such activities, everyone may be called upon to take an active part in performing in skits and in making fun during, for example, competitive games such as cricket. Everybody can recall having been called to the front of a village gathering and having to face the whole village as an unwilling victim of ritual humiliation. This may range from being blackened with charcoal or being drenched in water to being ordered to carry out acts deemed obscene by the winning side after these games. All such occasions, spontaneous or otherwise, have one thing in common, however, and that is that there is never an audience in the sense that no-one is permanently relegated to the position of spectator. Not even persons occupying the most dignified (*malulu*) positions such as a priest or a 'chief', can rest assured that they will not be made the topic of a skit, and certainly nobody can permanently avoid having to take part in one. Examples of such skits, where a 'chief' or a dignified visitor is made the butt of a joke, are occasions when the older women on Nukunonu armed with 'guns' (i.e. broomsticks) approached the members of the Council of Elders during a cricket match and 'shot' them. Or, during a gathering in the meeting house, when the women proceeded to 'marry' off the oldest of them to a visiting foreigner. The women wrapped the 'couple' in fine mats, simulated intercourse and made remarks about how the 'bride' would either need plastic surgery or else she would have to carry her breasts over her shoulders as they were so long and worn out. Needless to say, this kind of behaviour is in stark contrast to the etiquette demanded in everyday life.

On festive occasions, the sides of the village usually take turns in performing. In this way they momentarily provide an audience for the other side, while plotting their own next challenge in a continuous exchange of presentations (such as food, songs, dancing and clowning). Although everybody may occasionally take part in humorous performances, most people do not end up as recognised comedians or clowns. It is also the case that being recognised as an accomplished clown does not appear to combine easily with achieving positions of institutional power within village affairs.

The social space within which humorous performances are embedded is informed by a pattern of communication based on an immediacy of exchange between competing sides. These sides are conceptualised as similar and equal, and must not be confused with the complementary sides of the kin group. The pattern of communication associated with the similar, competitive sides, allows for reflexivity in a sense akin to that described by Bruce Kapferer (1986). An objectification or externalisation of social relations is achieved through ritualised events which allow for a momentary adoption of the perspective of that which is defined as other. In Tokelau this effect is achieved through dividing all participants in the festive occasions into two or more competing sides. These sides then take turns in performing skits, dances, speeches and so on. Each item presented by the competing sides may be seen as an expression of that side's relationship to the previous or to the subsequently performing side. It is delivered in the form of a playful challenge, which is then taken up and elaborated upon in the performance presented by the subsequent side. In this way a reflection on social relationships which are normally taken for granted in the course of everyday life, is encouraged through the communicative pattern prevalent in this kind of social space. As described above, this social space is prototypically contrasted with the communicational patterns in the social space of the *fono* (political meeting), where actions by definition are imbued with efficacy, and where no such reflexivity is encouraged.

The conjunction of the very serious and the humorous that the clown helps to bring about in humorous performances such as the *faleaitu* or 'house of spirits', represents an important check on the gravity represented by the institutionalised power structures. In this capacity, the voice expressed through these humorous performances may even be said to have gained new importance today, in a time where, as Hereniko notes, 'chiefs' of novel kinds proliferate (1994: 3).

Projecting an alternative model of selfhood through theatre

I shall now describe how a group of New Zealand Tokelauans attempted to stage a challenge to common conceptions of morality and selfhood, choosing the traditional venue of the clown to do so. For this purpose they have adopted the medium of what is called action theatre, popular theatre, or theatre for community development. I shall discuss how the form of the performance, that is, action theatre, resonated with the kind of social space that I have described as being the framework for humorous performances in Tokelau, namely 'things of no account'.

In Tokelau, political leadership has traditionally consisted of elders and/or family heads, all male. Their formal arena is the *fono* and decision-making procedures in such meetings is by means of consensus. In the last few years, as a result of pressure from the UN (through the New Zealand Administration) to decolonise, an inter-atoll assembly has been delegated governmental powers. As mentioned earlier, since the mid-1960s, many Tokelauans have migrated to New Zealand. Lately, as a result of people returning from overseas, the 'New Zealand experience' has started to filter into Tokelau society. The difference between life in New Zealand and in Tokelau, at least as it was in the early 1960s, can hardly be overstated.

The atoll environment is composed of a very narrow band of numerous islets that enclose a lagoon much like a string of pearls. The islets are partially protected from the vast ocean that surrounds the atoll by a coral reef. The land area totals between ten and twelve square kilometres, and none of the islets rise more than five feet above sea level. There is very little fertile soil, and the annual rainfall is irregular. In contrast, the sea area that belongs to Tokelau is large, about 290,000km^2, and is abundant in fish. On each of the three atolls, the population is concentrated on one islet on the western, leeward side of the atoll. This means that a population of about 1,500 people lives on approximately 2–3 square kilometres altogether.

All members of each village either have rights to land on the atoll or else are married to someone who has. Land is inalienable property in the sense that it is forbidden to sell land by law. The *kaiga* or extended families are the major property-holding units in Tokelau. A kin group is seen as founded by a couple and as being held together by opposite sex siblings. Tokelauans refer, loosely speaking, to the offspring on the brother's side as the 'male side'. The 'male side' or the side called *tamatane* then, consists of brother's sons and their offspring, including women. *Tamafafine* is the 'female side' of the kin group, consisting of sister's daughters and their offspring (including men). Status as *tamatane* and *tamafafine* determines the allocation of leadership positions and of rights and obligations among members. The *tamatane* side has power and authority over productive property and its use, that is, right to control land. The *tamafafine* side has the right to live on the land and to control and distribute the produce of cooperative enterprises and other property associated with the *kaiga*. The unity of the members of the *kaiga* is expressed through their joint exploitation of and attachment to specific land areas, that is, the area on which the family homestead is located, and coconut plantation areas on the outer islets.

In most mixed-gender public situations interaction is informed by two main principles: the avoidance behaviour associated with the brother/sister relationship serves to regulate interaction between the sexes, and the codes of respect associated with the hierarchy of age regulate interaction across generations. Interaction in more intimate settings, such as in the 'back' (*tua*) areas of the village, in the cook-houses, etc., and in single-sex gatherings is usually less circumscribed by these canons of etiquette and morality, and much joking and gossiping takes place in these less formal fora. In the 'front' (*mua*) areas of the villages and in formal situations, behaviour is very much oriented towards the presentation of what Levy (1973) has described for Tahiti as shining, fragrant, polished surfaces combined with a smiling, light-hearted, outgoing demeanour. Tokelauans talk about this aspect of their behaviour in terms of 'face', *mata*, and make moral evaluations of each other in terms of it.

The project of the theatre group was to present a challenge to the dominant way of conceptualising cultural identity. It did this by creating a performance intended to demonstrate how the practices represented as 'the Tokelau way', *faka-Tokelau*, with the tendency to foreground light, harmony and graceful avoidance behaviour mentioned above, are inevitably and intimately connected with the production of a darker side, backgrounded in the dominant discourse and related to issues culturally defined as egotistical or anti-social behaviour, such as open public expression of sexual desires, pain and conflict. The dualistic conception of selfhood implied by this image of a light (*ao*) and a dark side (*po*) is a part of Tokelau cosmology of long standing. The members of the theatre group were aware of this. However, they wished to challenge the common tendency to value harmony and avoid conflicts associated with this cosmology, as they claimed that this tendency made it easy for people to deny cases of abuse of power (ranging from incest to violence, etc.).

The initiative for this project arose in the Tokelau community in the Wellington area of New Zealand early in 1990. During Easter many New Zealand Tokelauans get together for sports tournaments and festive celebrations of their common identity. That year, some members of the community used this occasion as an opportunity to question their fellow Tokelauans about their feelings *vis-à-vis* such gatherings: whether they felt satisfied with the range of cultural expressions afforded by such occasions, or whether they could wish for more and new forms of communication. As a response to the answers they received, which in the main expressed a desire for more ways to learn about and keep in touch with Tokelau culture, they then announced publicly that they were to produce the first Tokelau drama, with the aim of exploring Tokelau history and culture. This information was given at various gatherings in the Wellington region, stating that anyone who wished to participate was welcome to do so. As a result of this, and after a while, the group stabilised with a core membership of ten actors. Of these, four were young, first-generation New Zealand-born Tokelauans. Five were middle-aged and members of a previously established Tokelau song group, and the last member was a slightly older woman with strong links to the Tokelau Women's Committee and the pre-school movement in New Zealand. One of the members of the song group, who generally played an important role in community life, and who was one of the main forces behind this project, had had some previous experience working with alternative theatre in New Zealand in the late 1970s and early 1980s. He approached a *palagi* Community Cultural Worker who had extensive knowledge of theatre production, and this man became the instructor for the group. One of the young cast members had also previously worked with this instructor in a project at the Teachers Training College about unemployment among Pacific islanders in New Zealand.

The first play this group produced, *Tagi*, was only performed in New Zealand, and presented Tokelau history from pre-contact times through the arrival of slave traders and missionaries, to the establishment of Tokelau communities in New Zealand. The aim of this presentation was twofold. First, and as a response to the interviews they had carried out during the Easter festival, the play was to present Tokelau history and culture in a new way for the members of the community who were not familiar with it, to counter what the members saw as 'cultural erosion'. Second, the group sought to challenge dominant conceptions of Tokelau history. In this play, they therefore contrasted the pre-Christian religious beliefs with Christianity, the dominant gender-role pattern and authority structure with matters such as sexual abuse, violence and street-kids, and the traditional stress on sharing and compassion with the issue of economic dependency. To raise such matters in a serious, explicit manner within the context of public, festive situations is definitely not common (in Tokelau or in New Zealand), and to do so can be said to run counter to all canons of Tokelau etiquette.

The actors shared a desire to explore their cultural identity, a will to experiment, and in doing so, the courage to challenge the relatively strong common consensus in the communities. Although their personal motivations for embarking on this quest varied, a common denominator may be found in the deeply felt need to find ways of expressing and articulating the particular concerns arising from the enormous changes Tokelauans have experienced during the last thirty years. In the face of the tendency to focus on the positive sides of the Tokelau way of life, to stress harmony and to downplay conflict, this group saw its task as one of mediation between the old and the young, by articulating common experiences which are normally not voiced. In short, they were searching for a more viable conception of selfhood that could help people to 'face up to the challenges of the here and now' as they put it.

In doing this the members of the theatre group were negotiating codes of behaviour in a manner that may be described as 'deep play' (in Geertz's sense [1973]). In challenging commonly held notions about cultural identity, the actors were, in a way, playing with fire. They needed more than the necessary blessing from the elders to present their plays. They were aiming to achieve general recognition of the issues raised in the plays, such as the existence of incest and abuses of power. In addition, the project was controversial and had the potential to affect negatively the statuses of the actors within the communities.

The name of the group came to be 'Tokelau te Ata'. This name was intended as a play on the English word theatre (*te ata*), but, true to the canons of Tokelau poetry it carries multiple meanings, some of which are: 'Tokelau, the image', or 'Tokelau, the dawn' or perhaps most poignantly, 'Tokelau, the reflection'. The choice of name demonstrates how the group saw itself as holding up a mirror for the Tokelau communities through the plays.

The group conceived the idea of making a tour to Tokelau. In applications for funding to support this tour, the project was called 'The indigenous people's return to the homeland'. In preparation for the tour to Tokelau, a second play, *Tima*, was begun. This play was to focus on the tension between the individualism of the larger New Zealand society and the communal, extended-family orientation in the Tokelau communities. Whereas the first play, *Tagi*, was produced for the Tokelau communities in New Zealand, *Tima* was produced with Tokelau in mind. This objective influenced the production process in interesting ways, as it led to confrontations and reflections over the differences between life in Tokelau and in New Zealand, and also between the images held of Tokelau by cast members and the reality of life in Tokelau in the 1990s (some of the members had not been back to Tokelau since the early 1970s).

The theme of *Tima* centred on the situation of women, particularly their role within the extended family (see Hoëm, in press). A very rudimentary sketch of this play is as follows: the main character, Tima, has been abroad to get an education, and she returns to Tokelau thinking that she is there for a holiday. Her family has other plans for her, however. They want her to get married and settle down in Tokelau to look after her elderly parents. She becomes desperate when she realises this. She tries to talk it out with her parents, but they tell her to shut up and be respectful and obedient. She attempts to get support from an aunt, who, while sympathetic to her pleas, advises her that Tokelau needs people with her experience. The aunt tries to present Tima's case at a meeting held by the extended family, but they will not listen to her either. Tima meets an old acquaintance who works as a teacher in the village, to whom she becomes romantically attached. He almost convinces her to stay and work in Tokelau, before they are discovered talking by her father, who beats up the teacher. Thoroughly disgusted by the situation, Tima wants to leave. She rejects her suitor, but at this point the village priest intervenes and orders her to do as her parents say. The play ends with her marrying the suitor chosen by her parents.

This play presents the main character as motivated by a desire for romantic love, and as concerned with defending her right to make her own choices. This individualistic model of selfhood is then pitted against the communal orientation of Tokelau, where acceptance of the demands made on her by her extended family is the norm, and is seen as an expression of *alofa*, that is, 'love', in this context more in the sense of placing the collective good above individual desires.

The form of this theatre then, is such that, at what is called 'the situation of maximal oppression', the audience is invited to intervene and change whatever they think is wrong or should or could be different with the story. The scenes of the play are then enacted again, according to the wishes of the audience, and if the audience agrees, the final scene is rerun, but this time with a song depicting women as powerful and as individuals in their own right. This procedure is developed with the intention to raise peoples' consciousness through making them aware of what, within the therapeutic and revolutionary frame of reference promoted by this form of theatre, is referred to as the underlying conflicts of the community. It is assumed by those advocating the use of this form of theatre that the process will lead to an empowerment of people, which will allow them to make (or demand) changes for the better in the running of community affairs.

While working on this play, some of the female performers experienced very strong emotional reactions when experimenting with possible scenarios. The starting point for the play was a strongly felt wish by the actors to, as they put it, 'tell the women of Tokelau to stop hiding'. During discussions, it transpired that they perceived the negative side of the behaviour of Tokelau women in general (both in New Zealand and in Tokelau) as being hypocritical and dishonest. They described women as not showing their true emotions, as manipulating, as gossips and as conformists. Scenes were tried out, such as: 'A group of women sit and work and gossip in a cooking house in Tokelau. An outsider comes, tries to learn and help with their work, but the women only discourage and ridicule her'. Or: 'A family is gathered. The father is an autocratic ruler, but the mother self-effacingly obeys him, even though he might be in the wrong'. Or: 'People coming to Tokelau from the outside walk on the road (which is one of the most public areas of the village), and being ignorant of the local customs, they talk loudly, the women wear clothes that expose their bare shoulders and legs', and so on. In other words these outsiders do not observe the proper etiquette, and the villagers respond with ridicule to isolate them.

During experimentation with alternative scenarios it became apparent that on the one hand, all the cast members had experienced such behaviour and had felt victimised because of it. The fact that they were all going to Tokelau only served to strengthen this feeling of intense discomfort, since they knew that they themselves would soon be exposed to this aspect of village life. On the other hand, they could also recognise themselves as occasionally being in the roles of oppressors and victimisers, and this naturally felt deeply unsettling. Parallel to this, the cast members began to realise that it would probably not be a very good idea to come to Tokelau with only a negative image of its collective way of life, based largely on their exposure to what they perceived as a higher degree of individual freedom in New Zealand society, and then to tell the people there what the group, as outsiders, thought that the people living in Tokelau should do about it.

There were some heated discussions which ranged from vehement defence of Tokelau etiquette and morality to total rejection of these codes of behaviour. The discussions, prompted by experimental enacting of the scenes, were cast in terms of 'masks'. The *palagi* instructor (commissioned by the group to help them create the plays) prompted the actors to pose questions such as 'What is the mask of the woman who is in control?', 'What is the religious mask?' and even 'What are the masks of the three atolls?' The immediate reaction, true to the women's initial intention of wanting to 'tell the women of Tokelau to be themselves', was that the message of the play should be 'for everybody to take off their masks'. However, this led to the intriguing question of 'What is behind the mask?'

At this point opinions started to differ. Whereas one woman said that she saw hiding behind the masks 'a very gentle Tokelauan', others stated that the masks are an integral part of social life; they are not only negative, but they contain and protect what is positive about life in Tokelau. The hermit crab, which cannot survive without its shell, was used as a metaphor. There is no indigenous concept of 'masks' in Tokelau culture. However, the notion of 'face', *mata*, as mentioned earlier, may be said to denote something akin to what we may call 'public personae'. In other words, when the group began experimenting with 'masks' or 'face', and enacted habitual ways of behaviour, in their search for alternatives they immediately came up against some very fundamental principles informing their sense of identity. We see here how the members of the group, while debating how to construct this play, were caught up in a discourse of authenticity (expressed as a demand that Tokelau people should be themselves) and individual choice (that is, between different codes of behaviour).[8] The members of the cast acting their role as incompetent outsiders were concerned with preserving their personal dignity *vis-à-vis* the villagers who respond with acts of ridicule and shaming. It is possible to analyse this contrast in terms of opposed conceptions of selfhood. In this perspective we may see the cast members as relating to a model of selfhood that implies a stress on personal dignity and individual choice, in contrast to which the villagers' merciless joking and shaming speaks strongly of a more collectivistic orientation.

Although some of the activists were aware that the experimentation with different roles, faces or masks had served to bring about an explicit confrontation between two different models of selfhood, and had such a confrontation as their explicit goal, many other actors did not. As one woman put it, 'I entered the group because I wanted to be a mother, because I am proud of being a mother. I wanted the community to see me that way, and I asked for such a role, but I didn't know that it would be this deep'. What she seemed to be saying was that she had not expected to have to question her desire to be a mother. Furthermore, she was deeply ambivalent about having to publicly question Tokelau conceptions of motherhood.

During the tour to Tokelau, it became even more apparent than it had been in New Zealand that the members of the theatre group were relating to a different frame of reference than the form of interaction and communication which is usually referred to as 'the Tokelau way'. Moreover, these codes of behaviour were precisely what they had agreed to challenge through the plays. As the following examples will illustrate, they were confronted with these differences on many levels during the tour (as are most Tokelauans who return to Tokelau after a stay overseas), both in their encounters with everyday life in Tokelau and as responses to their play. One immediate reaction to the play was that 'this is not the truth'. What people actually meant by saying this, differed. Some were of the opinion that individual scenes were incorrect. For example one scene depicts the enforced marriage, and some responded to this by saying that arranged marriage no longer occurs in Tokelau. Others seemed rather to say that the play did not refer to somebody they knew (as most skits or *faleaitu* do) and therefore they did not quite know what to make of it.

This mixed reception may be further illustrated by the following examples. Parts of the audience saw the play as a true story, in the sense that they thought that its characters were expressions of their personal beliefs and lifestyles, and this was by far the most difficult experience for the members of the group. For instance, following the previous night's performance, an old woman walked up to a man who played what he himself considered to be a role representing everything he hated about his culture, i.e. a Bible-loving patriarch oppressing his family. She said 'I was so happy to see that you have turned out to be such a good person. Your mother would have been proud of you'. He related this incident to us afterwards, saying that he did not have the heart to tell her that he had played this role with the intention of exposing this character as hypocritical and abusive. Other members of the group also experienced increasing difficulties in separating themselves from the role they were playing in the eyes of the community, so much so that when for example the woman playing the main female character reached her home atoll, she found it necessary to make a public statement saying that she was not her.

It was in fact striking during the performances in Tokelau how many of the elders, the old men who hold formal political power, were either absent or were seated in the dark outside the meeting house. In this way they managed not to miss out on the performance, while at the same time they avoided giving the event the explicit blessing which their presence would have communicated. Their decision to stay outside of the open-walled meeting house can be taken as an indication that they realised that the popular theatre performance was intended to be different from the common humorous performances. In other words, some of the political leaders recognised the group as communicating something more serious than just a playful challenge to their authority. Suddenly it was not clear, either to the actors or to some of the political leaders, just exactly who were the 'chiefs' and who were the 'clowns' in this venture.

These reactions reflect the difficulties people had with classifying this kind of performance. On the one hand, the performance seemed to be the same kind of social event as the traditional 'non-serious' humorous performances, but on the other hand it was equally obvious to many members of the audience that the alternative images of selfhood the theatre group projected were seriously intended. The topic of the play was a challenge to dominant codes of behaviour, and it was intended to help liberate both players and audience. On the other hand, this challenge was carried out within a particular social space provided by the very system they intended to challenge. In conclusion I shall comment a little further on the theoretical implications we may draw from our observation of this paradox.

Social spaces and human agency

During the Tokelau sojourn, the members of the group redefined their conceptions of what they were doing, from 'we are presenting information that we wish to convey for educational purposes', to local notions of festivity and prestation-exchanges. They moved from a framework where their perception of what they were doing was defined as to 'take a message to an audience' to one where they saw themselves as 'presenting a gift'. Their intention of projecting an alternative existence to the members of the community with the purpose of empowering them to make their own choices was gradually overshadowed by a rather different definition of situation. This new definition of what they were doing was clearly affected by the different pattern of communication proper to the kind of social space they were entering, and it was expressed as 'we are coming to Tokelau with a gift, to celebrate'. This is how the group came to present their intentions to the Council of Elders in Tokelau, when they were invited to attend its meeting at the beginning of their stay to explain the purpose of their visit. Conversely, on the community's side, the group's gift was accepted more as a total prestation, than as a contribution to further personal liberation and community development.

In other words, we see here how the local conceptions of what kind of social space an event is defined as, greatly influenced the impact of the activists' performance.

A turning point in the theatre group's process of redefining what it was doing was reached during a workshop teaching the methods of popular theatre to members of the community, mainly teachers, when the *palagi* instructor admonished potential actors 'not to become stuck in the clown'. His Shakespearean vision of a conflict-oriented theatre – of presenting a full blown tragedy in stark contrast to the Tokelau clown's concern with the minute details of everyday community life – suddenly seemed to the Tokelau actors to have the potential of undermining the social space that had allowed them to present their plays in the first place. At this point it became clear that, even though the activists in the group had an agenda of their own (namely to gain legitimacy for their new model of selfhood and thus indirectly to establish themselves as new political 'chiefs') they were not prepared to fight for the control of this social space in Tokelau in a way that they had had no qualms about doing when they presented the performances in New Zealand.

A reason for this is that their challenge to the authorities within the New Zealand communities had been strongly motivated by their dream about their homeland – 'the source' as they called it. When they arrived at 'the source' as guests, they experienced a strong pressure, but also a desire to adjust their vision accordingly.

I have related this story to provide an illustration of the experiential depth we may gain in our analysis of performance, if we shift our perspective from a singular focus on the products of performative activities, such as a drama or a skit, to a broader analysis of the production process itself. We have, on the one hand, seen that being exposed to the larger context of New Zealand society seems to have furthered a kind of introspective self-reflection in the actors, expressed as a concern with personal dignity, in contrast to which the Tokelau practice of shaming through joking and ridicule was experienced as acutely painful. It may also be argued that it was this exposure to the larger New Zealand society that brought about the desire to engage in political activism in the first place. On the other hand, we have also seen that the social spaces in which Tokelau humorous performances are embedded encourage its own form of reflexivity. However, this form of reflexivity demands an active participation in social relations, and follows the pattern of a gift- or prestation-exchange between sides that are defined as equal for the duration of the performance. Thus this kind of social space does not encourage or enforce a strict division between 'chiefs' and 'clowns'.

The models of selfhood (that is, a collective or relationally oriented model and another, more individualistic model) that may be inferred from the examples that I have presented above, have been variously described in anthropological literature in terms of broad contrasts such as 'honour and shame' versus 'guilt and dignity' oriented cultures. Furthermore they are frequently discussed in relation to processes of globalisation and modernity. These kinds of contrasts frequently do not rise above the level of simplistic contrasts between systems of morality. To counter this tendency I suggest that a possible way to go is to include in our analyses an awareness of the fact that conceptions of agency may vary qualitatively across social spaces, and that this factor also may affect communicational patterns significantly, even within a relatively homogenous community. In other words, this factor is also of utmost importance when it comes to analysing cultural movements such as the one engaged in by the group of political activists that I have described in this article.

Notes

1 See Turner and Bruner (1986) for an exposition of anthropological approaches to experience.
2 See Besnier (1995) for an alternative analysis of literacy.

3 It is possible to describe this group as a 'Tokelau diasporic community in New Zealand', following Smadar Lavie and Ted Swedenburg's (1996) definition of a diaspora as individuals who have dual identities and affiliations, both to a place of origin and to a place or places where they presently reside or formerly resided, cf. Mary M. Crain (this volume). However, I chose not to employ this term as it is still most commonly associated with situations of involuntary exile. Also, concerning the new generation of New Zealand-born Tokelauans, who also were represented in the theatre group, the nature of their attachment cannot be said to be one of allegiance to different places, as most of them do not have a relationship to the atolls. Their eventual dual affiliations are to the communities in New Zealand and to the relationships they may form with other segments of New Zealand society.

4 Wessen *et al.* (1992) give the number of the Tokelau population in New Zealand in 1982 as 4,118. New Zealand is the main site for Tokelau migrants, but there exist smaller Tokelau communities in Western Samoa, American Samoa, Australia, Hawaii and mainland USA.

5 Tokelau conceptions of men and women's relations to the spirits may on one level be seen as representing women as more passive than men. Women are represented as channels and recipients *vis-à-vis* the spirits, whereas men are represented as more actively able to control these forces. This may be attributed to men's dominance of the formal political institutions. On another level however, women, particularly in their role as sisters, through their channelling of the spirits' agency, may heal or destroy. In this capacity women are also perceived as active. The complementary nature of Tokelau conceptions of gender is discussed in Hooper and Huntsman (1975).

6 For a parallel ethnographic case, see Besnier (1995).

7 For further literature on ritual inversion see for example Douglas 1968; Stallybrass and White 1986; Barlow 1992.

8 I am grateful to Eduardo Archetti for this observation.

Bibliography

Barlow, K. (1992) ' "Dance When I Die!": Context and Role in the Clowning of Murik Women', in W. E. Mitchell (ed.) *Clowning as Critical Practice: Performance Humor in the South Pacific*, Pittsburgh PA and London: University of Pittsburgh Press.

Besnier, N. (1995) *Literacy, Emotion and Authority: Reading and Writing on a Polynesian Atoll*, Cambridge: Cambridge University Press.

Bloch, M. (1986) *From Blessing to Violence: History and Ideology in the Circumcision Ritual of the Merina of Madagascar*, Cambridge: Cambridge University Press.

Douglas, M. (1968) 'The Social Control of Cognition: Some Factors in Joke Perception', *Man*, 3: 361–76.

Friedman, J. (1994) *Cultural Identity and Global Process*, London: Sage.

Geertz, C. (1973/1993) *The Interpretation of Cultures*, Glasgow: Fontana.

——(1983) *Local Knowledge*, New York: Basic Books.

Gell, A. (1995) 'Closure and Multiplication: An Essay on Polynesian Cosmology and Ritual', in D. de Coppet and A. Iteanu (eds) *Cosmos and Society in Oceania*, Oxford: Berg.

Goffman, E. (1959) *The Presentation of Self in Everyday Life*, Harmondsworth: Penguin Books.

Hanson, F. (1982) 'Female Pollution in Polynesia', *Journal of the Polynesian Society*, 91: 335–81.

Hereniko, V. (1994) 'Clowning as Political Commentary: Polynesia, Then and Now', *The Contemporary Pacific*, 6, 1: 1–28.

Hoëm, I. (1995) *A Way With Words: Language and Culture in Tokelau Society*, Bangkok: White Orchid Press/The Institute for Comparative Research in Human Culture.

——(in press) 'Staging a Political Challenge: The Story of Tokelau te Ata', in V. Keck (ed.) *Common Worlds and Single Lives: Constituting Knowledge in Pacific Societies*, Oxford: Berg.

——(forthcoming) *A Sense of Place: The Politics of Identity and Representation*.

Hooper, A. (1993) 'The MIRAB Transition in Fakaofo, Tokelau', *Pacific Viewpoint*, 34, 2: 241–64.

Hooper, A. and Huntsman, J. (1975) 'Male and Female in Tokelau Culture', *Journal of the Polynesian Society*, 85: 257–73.

——(1996) *Tokelau: A Historical Ethnography*, Auckland: Auckland University Press.

Huntsman, J. (1971) 'Concepts of Kinship and Categories of Kinsmen in the Tokelau Islands', *Journal of the Polynesian Society*, 80: 317–54.

Kapferer, B. (1986) 'Performance and the Structuring of Meaning and Experience', in V. Turner and E. Bruner (eds) *The Anthropology of Experience*, Urbana and Chicago IL: University of Illinois Press.

Lavie, S. and Swedenburg, T. (eds) (1996) *Displacement, Diaspora, and Geographies of Identity*, Durham NC and London: Duke University Press.

Levy, R. I. (1973) *Tahitians: Mind and Experience in the Society Islands*, Chicago IL and London: University of Chicago Press.

Sahlins, M. (1985) *Islands of History*, London and New York: Tavistock Publications.

Schechner, R. and Appel, W. (1990) *By Means of Performance: Intercultural Studies of Theatre and Ritual*, Cambridge: Cambridge University Press.

Schieffelin, E. L. (1985) 'Performance and the Cultural Construction of Reality', *American Ethnologist*, 12, 4: 707–24.

Shore, B. (1982) *Sala' ilua: A Samoan Mystery*, New York: Columbia University Press.

——(1989) 'Mana and Tapu', in A. Howard and R. Borofsky (eds) *Developments in Polynesian Ethnology*, Honolulu HI: University of Hawaii Press.

Stallybrass, P. and White, A. (1986) *The Politics and Poetics of Transgression*, London: Methuen.

Turner, V. (1987) *The Anthropology of Performance*, New York: PAJ Publications.

Turner, V. and Bruner, E. (eds) (1986) *The Anthropology of Experience*, Urbana and Chicago IL: University of Illinois Press.

Valeri, V. (1985) *Kingship and Sacrifice: Ritual and Society in Ancient Hawaii*, Chicago IL: University of Chicago Press.

——(1990) 'Constitutive History: Genealogy and Narrative in the Legitimation of Hawaiian Kingship', in E. Ohnuki-Tierney (ed.) *Culture through Time: Anthropological Approaches*, Stanford CA: Stanford University Press.

Wessen, A. F., Hooper, A., Huntsman, J., Prior, I. A. M. and Falmond, C. E. (eds) (1992) *Migration and Health in a Small Society: The Case of Tokelau*, Oxford: Clarendon Press.

Chapter 3

From temple to television
The Balinese case

Felicia Hughes-Freeland

Indonesian State Television came into full operation in August 1962 and became available on the island of Bali in 1977, when the Indonesian government provided every subdistrict of Bali with a television set. Subsequently a long-term project, 'Television and the Transformation of Culture in Bali', was initiated. Since 1990 this project has been recording a number of television programmes broadcast in Bali (Hughes-Freeland 1992). In conjunction with commentaries by Balinese people, this documentation will serve as a resource to further our understanding of the subject-matter of television programmes, as well as television's social significance. This chapter draws on preliminary ethnographic findings from the project, and considers the more general conditions which bear on socio-cultural change.

The anthropological study of television raises questions about the nature of participation and identification, about the diffusion of media or virtual forms into 'real' life, about media's role as engaging ritual empowerment in specific groups, and about the process of redrawing the boundaries of identity. Faye Ginsburg has suggested that the focus on people's activities with media is the first step in a research process which should be more explicit in recognising that 'social bodies – from nation states to provincial communities to individuals – increasingly mediate and comprehend their identities and placement in the world in relation to televisual and cinematic structures and experiences' (1994a: 137; also Spitulnik 1993; Ginsburg 1994b). The analysis of media elicits contrasting approaches to 'people's activities' which anthropologists will be familiar with from debates about ritual activity: does ritual reinforce authority or does it provide a release from quotidien structure? In studies of the media, these alternatives are reproduced in current explanations of responses to the media, where members of the audience tend to be treated as passive pawns or active readers (Hughes-Freeland 1997).

This dichotomy is also represented in approaches to social identity, which became an important theme in cultural studies and also, by the 1990s, in social science. There are two contrasting theories of social identity, modelled on idioms of performance and consumption respectively. The performative version has been associated with dramaturgical and ritualised accounts of social action (Geertz 1973; Turner 1974) and comes to rest in an emphasis on experience, on lived reality. In an extreme form, identity is seated in individual consciousness, rooted in experience and agency (Cohen 1994). Performative approaches however have not focused exclusively on the individual, but have also taken collectivist approaches (Hughes-Freeland 1998). The consumptative version of identity has been fuelled by the anxieties of the Frankfurt school about a loss of authenticity resulting from technologies of replication, and came to rest in an emphasis on simulacra, or hyperreality (Baudrillard 1988). Approaches referring to this idiom are collectivising approaches to experience. In world systems theory, for example, identity tends to be discussed in terms of consumption in a collectivist idiom. The actor perspective is irrelevant to historical processes of secularisation or detraditionalisation in which the social experience of ritual and media corresponds to two distinct ideal phases (Friedman 1994). In an individualist analysis (such as Cohen 1994), both ritual experience and media become means to being: sites for the generation of action and meaning which are both the cause and effect of identity. However, in both cases, the theorisation of identity rests on a notion of power. In the first, power, like water, flows down; in the second, power, like grass, grows upwards from the roots. The problem is how to bring these two perspectives into a single analytical framework.[1]

This problem is recognised in anthropology's theoretical endeavour to explain social phenomena with reference to both structure and agency. The anthropological approach to understanding the place of television in the construction and transformation of social identity attempts to overcome such dichotomies by engaging with both perspectives. I propose here to consider wide-reaching questions about identity and the representation of culture with reference to two versions of a specific performance of an *arja* play; one was performed at a temple festival, the other was recorded in a television studio without an audience for broadcast on the Balinese station of Indonesian State Television (TVRI). In this chapter, performance will refer to the specific events in the form of two *arja* plays, and I will provide a performative analysis of the responses to the two plays. In this way the research into Balinese television will explore the crisis of identity – and indeed the crisis of how to theorise identity in the light of the two approaches outlined above.

After outlining the background to perceptions of Balinese cultural identity, I give a brief ethnography of the *arja* play in its two perfor-mance contexts, and then turn to the commentaries elicited from Balinese viewers as they watched the performances. These responses constitute a specific instance of Balinese media practices in the form of local responses to the documentation of traditional performance on television in order to explore perceptions of differences between live and broadcast performance, but I will suggest broader structural constraints and determinations which bear on such practices. I conclude with some suggestions about what anthropology specifically can contribute to the proliferating literatures about television and society. The chapter suggests that if we consider identity as based on *doing* rather than on *being*, we will restore issues of agency and social roles to our conceptualisation of identity, and move away from the images and stereotypes which result from an understanding of identity as *being*.

Identifications of Balineseness

What is Balinese identity? In order to understand the relationship of television to Balinese society, it is useful to have an understanding of stereotypic images of Bali, images which have been challenged by recent research on Bali and Balineseness. ' "Bali" refers simultaneously to an island, a province, an ethnic group' (Picard 1996: 150). The impact of tourism and modernisation on the Indonesian island of Bali has produced a literature which reveals how 'Balineseness', the identity of Bali, has been constituted by a number of stereotypes or images promoted by scholars, artists, the Indonesian government, tourists, Balinese cultural brokers and others. Although Balinese identity can be situated in the actions of Balinese people as members of an ethnic group, Balineseness has more usually been present as an *image*, produced by non-Balinese, with varying degrees of input by the Balinese people themselves.

Three dominant images of Bali have been prevalent.

Bali is outside history

Balinese society has been presented as a hermetic space, sealed off from external trends such as Islam and colonialism which characterise the historical development of neighbouring Java. The religious practices of Bali have been read as the surviving remnants of the Javanese Hindu-Buddhism which was ousted from Java by the spread of Islam since the fourteenth century, and Bali has been presented as a museum of pre-Islamic culture. This image was initially fostered by Dutch colonial policies towards Bali, and has been sustained, even intensified, in the Indonesian promotion of Bali as an international tourist destination. Bali, then, has come to represent tradition incarnate, exotic and authentic, outside history, in another dimension (Fabian 1983).[2]

Bali is the island of the gods

This is the most usual label applied to Bali. No one visiting the island can fail to be struck by the temple ceremonies in which offerings are made to the invisible forces which sustain life. The community busily makes offerings of food, prays, and watches the various performances offered to the gods who have been invited down to the temple for the duration of the festival. The offerings are spectacular and labour-intensive, made of mounds of aesthetically processed foodstuffs piled high on small round trays which are balanced by women on their heads as they carry them to the temple, often in long community processions. Coordinated by the community association (*banjar*), these processions are performances in themselves, with different subsections of the community wearing different coloured jackets and sashes. This repetitive cycle of religious activity across the island has contributed to the image of Balineseness as one of harmonious spirituality expressed in an artistic and sensual (non-Islamic) style.

All Balinese are performers and artists

Ethnographically, the performative image of Balinese identity has been reinforced by community participation in colourful temple ceremonies. The remark by an early expatriot resident in Bali, the Mexican artist Miguel Covarrubias, 'Everyone in Bali seems to be an artist' (1937: 160), has contributed to the idealised image of the Balinese as being inherently creative. The famous book on dance and drama (1938) by the English dance critic Beryl de Zoete and the German painter Walter

Spies was one of the first detailed studies of non-western performance and consolidated this image of Bali as a haven of aesthetic and hedonistic bliss. The anthropologists Gregory Bateson and Margaret Mead joined the expatriot circle in Bali in the 1930s while they made a study of Balinese culture and personality which equated Balinese personal and social identity with the image of artist and performer (1942).[3] To this day, it is the image of the young female dancer which remains the dominant icon of Bali, an icon used to market package holidays to Bali and also to other parts of Indonesia.

These three images are the product of outsiders coming to Bali and describing it to an outside audience. They suggest that Bali has a unbroken and homogenous tradition of social harmony, expressed in temple rituals, and that outside visitors have had no impact on the processes which constitute 'Balineseness'. From this perspective, socio-economic changes resulting from the tourist industry and exposure to imported and home-grown mass media threaten an antique and authentic culture, and are therefore dangerous. Thinking about television in this version of Bali is to conjoin one of the most intensely and uniquely exoticised societies in the world with one of the world's most reductive and allegedly homogenising technologies. The arrival of television in Bali in 1977 may indeed seem a socio-cultural anomaly, if we persist in thinking of Bali as an unspoiled island paradise, and conceptualise cultures like this as insular totalities, until only recently out of history and out of contact.

This conceptualisation is of course false, and these illusory though compelling identifications of Bali are being challenged, just as the structural-functionalist model of culture has been challenged. Postcolonialism and globalisation have produced critiques which make the objectification and reification of culture at once more patently false, and, paradoxically, more patently promotable: illusions of cultural others gain currency precisely because of the globalisation which makes their otherness more illusory by the day. In the case of Bali, the critique of the earlier images – which none-the-less continue to feed the images market – may be summarised as follows.

Bali has always been in history and in contact

The image of Bali as immune from history is the result of colonial image-making (Schulte Nordholt 1986). Throughout history, the idiom expressing the relationship between political and religious insti-

tutions within Bali has varied (Reid 1993). What appear to be traditional systems of law, social organisation and religion are forms of
rationalisation introduced by the government of the Dutch East Indies.
They have been continued, and even intensified, since the recognition
of the Indonesian Republic in 1950 (Warren 1991).

Bali is heterogeneous

By the time the Dutch gained control of the island, Bali was divided into
eight rival kingdoms. These kingdoms were traditional rivals, but after
the pacification of Bali and its subsequent integration into the
Indonesian Republic, Balinese people continued to celebrate regional
variation between local communities (*banjar*) and administrative
districts (*kabupaten*), in the form of competitions in dramatic and
sporting events. Bali has not only been internally divided in a self-
conscious way which imbues individuals with a specific sense of local
belonging. The island has also been settled by non-Balinese, especially
Javanese people, and in the northern ports of Bali in particular there has
been a strong Islamic influence (Wikan 1990). Bali has been an island of
schemers and power-mongers as much an island of the gods, of slave-
traders and profiteers. For example, the first tourists were brought to
Bali to fill ships which had transported pigs to Singapore (Vickers
1994). Today, Balinese people are also Indonesian citizens, and struggle
to pursue their interests with reference to more than one 'imagined'
community, as well as their own immediate families and communities.

To be Balinese is not necessarily to be a performer or an artist

The stereotypical identity of Balinese as thespian aesthetes has been
questioned by a number of researchers (Hobart 1985a; Wikan 1990;
Jensen and Suryani 1992; Vickers 1996). They argue, in their different
ways, that what to westernised eyes might appear ritualised behaviour
with a distinct cultural pattern is not an appropriate representation of
what Balinese people say and do, and reveals more about practices
originating in the West than in Bali. Painting or dancing in Bali is not
who you *are*, they are activities which you may or may not *do* at particular times and places. Balinese individuals and groups are agents, or are
invested with the power to do, and the identity which derives from
doing, by participating in different situations (Hobart 1995).

These three revisions of Balineseness reveal the importance in Bali's history of political and economic contact – with others, especially with the Javanese and other Indonesian societies, the Dutch, and more recently, fellow-Indonesians and international tourists. Previous stereotypes would indicate that Bali is changing from a localised and traditional society to a modern, globalised one, but recent research indicates that Bali has been part of a global system for a long time, and would not be Bali were it not for its relations with non-Balinese over time.

Balineseness and externality

Balineseness then, is constituted by relations with non-Balinese. A recent trend in understanding culture has been to see it in two ways: first as a dynamic process of hybridisation, and second as something constituted from an external vantage point (see Crain, this volume). These arguments have been applied to Bali with regard to tourism, as something which is not destructive of culture, but constitutive of it (McKean 1989); Balinese 'culture' has resulted from a process of hybridisation, and accounts of Balinese 'culture' remain hybrid.

This hybridisation is part of Balinese experience and creativity over time, but the effect of interaction with non-Balinese has been a problem for other outsiders. Vickers has noted how, in the 1930s, De Zoete's typology of Balinese performance could not easily accomodate forms which combined Balinese and Malay influences, such as *kebyar* music, *stamboel* plays, and *janger* dances (Vickers 1996: 19–24). These appropriations, hybrids and innovations are intrinsic features of Balinese culture (Picard 1996), and today – perhaps ironically – it is the *kebyar* style which represents Balinese music in the world music scene to non-Balinese, and to Balinese living outside Bali.

Bali's restoration to a total or global history has made it possible to understand how much its identity as a paradise associated with performance and spirituality is an image which has been created and compounded by outsiders, such as the painter Walter Spies and the impresario John Coast (Coast 1954; Vickers 1989; Pollman 1990). These 'expats' not only consumed Balinese culture, but produced some of its most enduring forms which signify Balineseness – such as the Barong and Kris dance and the Kecak or Monkey dance (Picard 1996) – and were the first marketeers of the Balinese cultural experience for a translocal market.

The process whereby Balinese culture is represented to the outside world by scholars may also express a process of hybridised cultural interaction. Recently, for example, a book on Balinese performance by an American and a Balinese classifies Balinese performance on a sacred–profane axis, in relation to contexts ranging from inner temple to commercial (Bandem and deBoer 1995). This draws on the earliest typology of Balinese performance by Tyra de Kleen, published in 1921, which distinguished sacred performance from the secular, and the spiritual from the pleasurable (Picard 1996: 122–4), a distinction made famous by Beryl de Zoete.[4]

These factors have led Vickers to suggest that Balinese modernity has been not a homogeneous but a heterogeneous process:

> Modernity was not a thing which any one group could own in itself, but the sense of being modern was given specific forms in Bali. By being able to articulate this sense in such forms as didactic theatrical speech, or as incongruous costumes, or as exciting music, Balinese could become agents of change.
>
> (Vickers 1996: 22)

So there are different ways of thinking about Balineseness. This identity includes – and, some would claim, subsumes – externality in the form of heterogeneous agencies and interests from outside. It is therefore possible that the arrival of television in Bali does not represent such a unique or iconoclastic incursion as it might at first appear. Instead, like tourism, it may be responded to flexibly, resiliently, and keep Balinese culture alive, a point to which I will return below.

Having outlined the notional idea of Balineseness, I will turn to the particulars of ethnographic data. First I will briefly describe two versions of an *arja* play, and then I will analyse the responses of two Balinese men to these versions, to allow me to evaluate one way in which television engages with Balinese society – or, how two Balinese individuals engage with television. As already noted, participation in social situations is contingent on where an individual fits in to a group, but fitting in is part of a process which cannot simply be accounted for by the implementation of clear-cut rules which determine behaviour and choice absolutely and predictably; there is a performative dimension to fitting in. The following ethnography forms part of an effort to ungeneralise Bali and Balineseness, and illustrates how my respondents distinguished between ritual and television. I will then consider the implications of these distinctions, and conclude with some general comments about explaining social transformation.

The play

During 1991, an *arja* play, *Keris Pusaka Sakti*, which can be translated roughly as *The Blessed Bequested Blade*, was broadcast every week from 6–24 June in four episodes of about one hour each. *Arja* is a form of theatre which combines singing, dancing, speaking and repartee. Most Balinese would be familiar with *arja* from performances at temple festivals. Classified as a 'secular dance of the outer temple' (Bandem and deBoer 1995: 79–82), it is more than entertainment for human eyes, and has a 'traditional' association with events that have come to stand for quintessential Balinese culture.

Arja has stock characters with their own language and movement styles. The plots usually involve two courts. Each court has two male attendants, one large and one small (Penasar and Wijil in each case), and a female maid (Condong and Desak respectively), all of whom are comic characters. Other comic characters are Liku and Limbur, who in the story below play the Princess and Queen in the 'ignorant' kingdom of Metaum, and the Crown Prince (Mantri Buduh), played by a woman. The other kingdom (Jenggala) has a King (Raja Manis), played by a woman, and a Queen (Galuh). When these royals sing, the Penasar will explain what they have been singing about. These comic characters enliven the action and mediate between their superiors and the audience.

The plot of *Keris Pusaka Sakti* is as follows:

1   The Crown Prince of Metaum is in love with Galuh, but in a contest for her hand, the King of Jenggala is the victor. The Prince still loves Galuh, and his sister Liku is in love with Galuh's husband, Raja Manis, the King of Jenggala.
2   While the King is away hunting, the Crown Prince visits Jenggala and falls in love again with the Queen. He tries to persuade her to go away with him, but she refuses.
3   Back in Metaum, the Queen plans to have a tooth-filing ceremony as an excuse to bring the Jenggala couple to Metaum to satisfy her offspring's amorous longings. The King comes on his own, amid much small talk and banter, and refreshments are served. The King drinks a cup of drugged coffee, a love potion which makes him think that he is in love with Liku. His male attendant tries to break up the ensuing amorous behaviour and is beaten off by the King, who thrashes him.

4   The male attendants from Jenggala decide to go home to tell the
     Queen what has happened. On hearing the news she is distraught,
     and fetches the heirloom of her birthplace, the dagger of the
     kingdom of Daha.

5   The Queen arrives at Metaum with the dagger, and fights with
     Liku. Her bewitched husband fails to recognise her. When she
     reminds him that she is his wife, he attacks her. The skinny
     Jenggala attendant attacks Liku, who is defended by her maid and
     the King. The Queen falls weeping to her knees before her
     husband. He is enraged, and pulls out his own dagger, the heir-
     loom of Jenggala. They fight. Then comes a voice from the
     invisible world which declares that the King has been bewitched.
     By bringing together the two blades of their two daggers, they can
     defeat the powers of Metaum.

6   The play ends rapidly with a reconciliation. The thwarted Liku
     weeps loudly, driving the newly conscious King, yet again, to
     attack her.

The play about the play

The television version of this play was staged in a studio without an
audience and performed by the Denpasar Indonesian State Radio *arja*
troupe.[5] After discussion with the project household, it was decided
that this was the best of the *arja* plays broadcast on television, and
Mark Hobart made arrangements to sponsor the same play by the
same troupe at a temple festival due to take place at a time when we
could both be in Bali to document it. And so it came about that in
August 1992 I videoed the same troupe performing the same play with
(mostly) the same cast as part of the annual temple festival (*piodalan*)
at the Duwur Bingin lineage temple in the ward of Tengahpadang; that
version was longer than the television version, and lasted about five
hours. I then watched this recording with Balinese people who had
already seen the television version more than once, in order to elicit
commentaries from them.

'The' Balinese audience in this case consisted (mainly) of two
people: Ktut, a commoner, and Gung Kak, a noble. I say mainly
because other members of the household, such as Ktut's son and
daughter-in-law, occasionally joined us and added to the discussion.
When the research took place, Ktut was in his early fifties, and Gung
Kak in his eighties. Despite the difference in their age and rank, Ktut
and Gung Kak have a close friendship based on shared thespian pasts,

fostered by a sense of mutual obligation. Gung Kak had specialised as a performer and teacher of *arja* until 1962, whereas Ktut had dabbled in *janger* and modern *derama* until the 1970s. These two men thus had long-established interests in performance and culture. They took considerable pride in their artistic pasts, and also derived enormous pleasure from reminiscing about various incidents, together and with me. I formed the third member of the audience: anthropologist, English, middle-class, university lecturer, in her late thirties. My present interests were similar to those of Ktut and Gung Kak, but came out of a different past and were directed to future results which would be relevant outside Bali, rather than influencing future situations in the Balinese household. I was a transient player, passing through the ongoing relationship between Ktut and Gung Kak.

These commentaries resulted from a play of interests, and to a certain extent, Balinese men playing with the younger anthropologist. The commentaries constitute what might be seen as a clash of discourses: local Balinese world views meet infra-local media representations. Balinese people tend to talk about things in a less essentialising manner than British or American anthropologists (Hobart 1985b). This particular form of pragmatism is demonstrated not only in how Balinese people rationalise the world in conversation, but also in the ways they integrate ritual into their everyday life, and in the ways they talk about television. However, these commentaries are more appropriately seen as testimonies to the imponderabilia of cultural response (to amend Malinowski's well-known phrase), and also to its unpredictability. The three of us had different assumptions and expectations which became clear in the activity of elicitating interpretations in front of the television set. For anthropologists, ritual, performance and media are helpful concepts for challenging objectivist views of reality so as to allow us to understand how realities are constructed (Hughes-Freeland 1998). In this particular situation, these different concepts were being brought into play in a Balinese style, albeit catalysed by a western academic project. The resulting situations turned out to be, as it were, doubly deconstructive.

The commentaries

In the commentaries elicited at viewings of recordings of both versions of the play, Ktut and Gung Kak made a number of predictable comments.

Live performance is livelier   Both men agreed that the performers of *arja* at the temple had stronger movements (*ambek*) and more energy (*eseh*) because of the presence of the audience. The audience enhanced the stage presence of the actors.

Live performance gives comic actors more space to establish their characters   The conventional sequences where characters talk about themselves and their problems (*angucap-ucap*) are longer in live performances than on television. As these sequences are usually highly comical, there is an impoverishment in the television version.

Comic language is freer in live performance   This follows on from the previous point. For example, in the temple performance, one joking scene was based entirely on sexual puns. The television version by contrast used jokes to communicate advice on development issues such as family planning. There was a transformation from entertainment to edification.

Television relies more on dialogue than improvised gesture and action   In the televised version of the play, verbal skills were given more emphasis than embodied ones. The two treatments of the reconciliation scene early in the play also illustrates the previous points.

We see a row between the King and his wife the Queen who is upset because of her husband's prolonged absences on hunting expeditions. The row is observed by three comic characters: the two male attendants and the female maid. The performance of the reconciliation in the television version was expressed entirely through spoken language. By contrast, in the live performance, spurred on by the audience, the skinny male attendant picked up the struggling maid physically and embraced her, to the uproarious delight of the audience (and the other actors).

Ktut said that such a display of physical contact between a man and a woman would be frowned on in daily life but it is quite common in *arja*, although not in televised versions. I found the television scene exceedingly dull, especially after seeing the live version which (for me) was the high point of the performance.

As both commentators prided themselves on their practical and general knowledge of theatre, it is not surprising that the commentaries focused on performance technique and stagecraft. Nor is it surprising that Ktut and Gung Kak did not always make the same point or agree with each other; for example, they disagreed over whether the conventional invocation of kingly virtues in the first Jenggala scene was better live or on television. Their friendship feeds on affectionate competition, and personal feelings also influenced their commentaries. Ktut kept referring to a mysterious falling out with the actress playing the Crown Prince in the live performance which happened some thirty years ago; his judgements of her performance tended to be somewhat more uncharitable than Gung Kak's. These comments tell us about the particular personal interests of the two men, which would not be shared by every Balinese.

What was unpredictable was their preference for the artistry of the televised version of the play to the liveliness of the temple perfor-mance. For example, the movement transitions (*angsel*) which require good signalling between the dancers and the drummers were better in the television version than in the temple performance. Although Gung Kak preferred the live performance because you could see the performers better – and at this point, Gung Kak was suffering from cataracts – he argued that the quality of dancing in general was better on television. The actors were more assured and certain because they would be filmed, and become an exemplar (he used the Indonesian word *contoh*). In the live performance, the actors did not concentrate properly on their performance because they were distracted by the audience. The situation encouraged them to make jokes and to play to the audience, instead of concentrating on the dancing.

Both Ktut and Gung Kak concluded that the energy of the live performance spoilt the dancing. An excess of energy (*eseh*) removes the *taksu*. It is difficult to translate *taksu* because it forms part of a system of evaluations used to interpret and analyse the aesthetics of perfor-mance practice in different performance contexts. In this context, I will simply gloss it as power of the performance endorsed by supernatural forces.

To the anthropologist, who was tending to impute greater authen-ticity to a live performance with an audience than one in a studio performed for the cameras, this evaluation was difficult to accept. It is true that both men missed the interaction of audience and performers in the television version. None-the-less, an important element of performative power, *taksu*, was considered to be more at risk from interactions with the audience in the temple festival than from what I had seen as the barren alienation of the television studio. There was no sense that the formalisation of the broadcast might secularise the performance and remove its *taksu*, or contain the performance's energy in a negative way.[6] The converse was true. The artistry was enhanced.

What seemed to be emerging from the conversations about the two performances was a distinction between an aesthetic response and one of pleasure. The television version scored on traditional cultural values, but the live version rated for the fun of the language and the interactive role of the audience. Inherent in the view of the television performance is the notion of exemplar: the performance is recorded, and will be seen repeatedly. It will be used as a measure of the standard of the performance, and thus of Balinese culture. Indeed, *arja* and a number of other traditional forms had been losing popularity to *sendratari*, a less inter-referential and technically complex form of dance-drama which was developed in the State Academies of the Performing Arts in Java and Bali in the 1960s. Television has been one means used in the 1990s to promote and preserve *arja* as a part of Balinese culture by members of the Balinese Academy of Performing Arts (Hughes-Freeland 1992, 1995).

From the Balinese point of view, then, television broadcasts were not threatening tradition, but sustaining it. Television performances are exemplars of Balineseness which are fitting for passing on Balinese standards of skill to the younger generation. This supports Caldarola's argument (1994) that there is a tendency to see televised performance in terms of artistry. This is not a *simulation* of ritual, but rather an extrapolation of an aspect of behaviour which forms part of ritual events – a focus on skill.

Balinese pragmatism versus western academic essentialism

There was a further twist to the discussions generated by this attempt to make distinctions between contexts, which illustrates an important point. Gung Kak rejected the clear-cut distinction between 'live' and 'broadcast'. He had not perceived the video version of the live performance as standing in *direct contrast* to the television one. We were, after all, commenting on a *recorded* version of a live performance. In addition, the production of the recording itself had altered the live performance: the video camera of the anthropologist made the dancing better in the live performance than it might have been had I not been documenting it. What Gung Kak's perception made clear was that the anthropological presence, represented by the video work, had moved the live performance into a midway position, between temple and television.

Apart from asserting the positive role of television in sustaining Balineseness through the broadcasting of traditional performance, then, the important point that the commentaries by Ktut and Gung Kak reveal about the relationship between temple and television is this: that what constitutes an event culturally is less clear-cut than general discussions about media versus so-called unmediated reality suppose. More often than not, Balinese temple performances are viewed by at least one video eye, normally in the hands of an Indonesian or international tourist. What Gung Kak's remarks showed is the error in thinking of live performance as authentic in an absolute way: there may be factors which inflect the style of performance from an interactive one to a more aesthetically conscious one. And in a studio situation, performers may attend more closely to the perfection of their art, freed from the participation of the audience.

Just as media representations are imagined as virtual, so conversely, does authenticity become an illusion. The action of Balinese stereotypes on the ethnographer's assumptions about authentic cultural experience is (again) illustrated in this fieldwork episode, as is the flexibility of the commentators to move between frames of reference, which suggests that the traditional and the 'modern' are not opposites, but part of the same structure.[7] It could be argued that the events depicted on television and in the temple are both equally subject to being interpreted as real and unreal as the other. And both are attempts to do something in the world.

The data show that the interaction between the audience of three and the television was used by the two Balinese men to assert their personal and social roles in relation to the programmes for the anthropologist as well as for each other. The social effect of mediating live performance by video recording and studio performance by television could be characterised as a rite of affirmation of personal identity. At this level, then, the media representation affirmed who they were in an intensely individualistic way as well as according to their social status. At the same time, the intensity of this affirmation was itself the product of anthropological investigation. The attention paid to this particular *arja* play was beyond the normal call of culture, and the answers were wrought out of an interaction, not observed at a distance. The elicitation in itself was a major cause of data. The affirmation of Balinese identity was catalysed by the interests of the outsider, in a particular situation. At the same time, going against the grain of generalised

Balineseness as a collective identity, Balinese identities relate to activities and roles in situations; Balinese people have many cross-cutting roles. The identity game being played here was between three players, one of whom was less certain of the game than the other two, whose uncertainty compelled them to make more explicit than they might some of their own presuppositions. The play we were playing was a reprise of the importance of externality in the construction of Balineseness.

Long-term trends?

The argument thus far suggests that television, like tourism, is perhaps enhancing Balineseness, rather than undermining it. Bali survives because it changes, adapts and appropriates. While it is relatively simple to document audience responses ethnographically, we can conclude from the above that it is rather more difficult to generalise from these in order to tackle the broader structural picture proposed by Ginsburg above. The proliferation of micro-studies on local responses to or appropriations of different forms of media could, in principle, be compared to arrive at general patterns. However, there is a difficulty in so doing because each case is itself in a process of rapid transformation. In the case of the Bali project, it is premature to assess television's role in transforming 'Balineseness', but it is possible to identify some problems in dealing with these kinds of social processes. There are a number of factors which might stretch this adaptability and curtail local agency in the long term.

Global markets

The effects of globalisation on Bali are currently better documented with regard to tourism than media. In a paper given to a conference in Australia in 1995, George Aditjondro (n.d.), an Indonesian academic and activist in semi-exile, detailed the ownership of companies investing in Balinese hotels and golf courses. These companies were not Balinese but Indonesian, and a large number were traced back to the family of President Suharto. One implication of this suggests that there is an inverse relation between Balineseness at the cultural level and the material: that the image-effect of symbolist culture operating on one level conceals those political and economic processes operating on another level, which undermine Balinese participation in controlling Balinese culture and Balinese resources.

Time and money

Television is only one element in a changing equation in the budgeting of time and money. Temple performances have traditionally been funded through the operation of shared community costs, but households are now being required to pay for tickets with money, marking a transition from a traditional exchange system to one which includes capitalisation (see below). Other changes in Bali are releasing time: for instance, the walls marking compound boundaries are now being made of breeze blocks or cement instead of dried mud thatched with *lalang* grass. Ktut explained that these new walls require considerable cash inputs initially, but they subsequently incur fewer recurrent labour costs than the traditional ones. Changes of this order interlock into a system where decisions have to be made about resourcing new ways of doing things. Television sets cost money, and they use up time.

Time and doing

Whereas the content of what is on television is analysed, it is television's potential to take time away from other communal activities which may be more important.[8] Balinese identity and agency is based in activities in particular situations. Their television viewing which started in the context of their membership of the ward round the village head's television set is now part of household situations (and research ones). It has been noted that when television arrives, it takes up time that would otherwise be spent doing other things. Ultimately it is economic interests or necessities, not television, which shapes the use of time. Modern work practices put pressure on the Balinese to spend less time and money on ritual. This policy began to have impact in Java in the late 1970s, but its effect (or effectiveness) in Bali remains to be seen.[9] One possibility is that in villages, modern work patterns will affect the younger generations, but those of Ktut and Gung Kak's age will continue to have time for ritual work. However, in the early 1990s, the ward still had legitimate claims on the time of its members to do community work, ritual work, sport and performance, all of which impinged on the time of those community members. More often than not, in the 1990s Balinese people watched television while working – or, paradoxically, when asleep – and are still more likely to watch television together than they are to eat together. Nonetheless, televising has the potential to change the amount of time spent with others. Ktut liked to watch the 10 p.m. international news, which he often did alone, when others were asleep. What will be interesting to see is whether or not television viewing results in more time being spent in the household, and whether or not this causes a shift in the community structure, away from the cross-cutting bases of identity to the nuclear couple with the concomitant reduction of female agency from sister and daughter to wife, as it has occurred in Malaysia (Rudie 1994).

Homogenisation of standards of excellence

The Balinese pride themselves on their own local community identity, and competition between communities has produced a thriving and diverse artistic ethos on the island. However, there has been a considerable reduction in the number of troupes; for instance, in the mid-1970s there were thirty-six *derama gong* troupes in two subdistricts alone, whereas now there are perhaps less than six in the whole of Bali (deBoer 1996: 170). One hypothesis being tested in the Balinese television project is that troupes who appear on television tend to secure more bookings by temple festival committees. These troupes, such as the Indonesian State Radio Arja Troupe, become star troupes. The result is that these star troupes put other troupes out of business, and the long-term effect will be a decline in the local variation which has been a feature of Balinese culture. There is already professionalisation of temple performance which is affecting the community at large. As of July 1992, every household in the Pisangkaja ward was required to buy a ticket for the show at the temple, whether they attend or not, ostensibly to meet the rising costs of the more famous troupes (cf. deBoer 1996: 169). It is significant that the Balinese in the project household picked troupes sponsored by state institutions – state radio for *arja*, and the Badung subdistrict police force for *derama gong* – as the best examples of televised performances of each theatrical form. This raises the question of whether the excellence associated with these institutions implies an emergent state hegemony in the performing arts, a question which for now cannot be answered.

Transforming instrumentality

Balinese ritual and theatrical performance differ in their intentions. Ritual is an act which intends to *change* the state of affairs in this world (Hildred Geertz in Wikan 1990: 315). Theatre, by contrast, enacts history which is understood to be truth (Hobart 1991). However, having said that, televised theatre is seen as an exemplar of Balinese action, and as such has a seriousness beyond pleasure in a simple sense of instant gratification. At this level, then, it has an instrumentality beyond entertainment, a ritual-like instrumentality which has hitherto been the preserve of the temples and priests, and this instrumentality lies in the Balinese perception that the state is using the media to produce and sustain a sense of local Balinese identity within the context of Indonesian national identity.

For my Balinese audience, nationalism is already in place, despite the rhetoric of opposition between Bali and Java, where Java stands metonymically for the state, i.e. Indonesia. The older audience of two are nationalists. They see television as serving to teach the young, who have not been through the bitter experience of violent struggle, to learn Indonesian-ness and Balineseness, and also as a way of teaching non-Balinese living in Bali about Balinese culture (Hughes-Freeland 1995). What they did not address in their discussions is the language issue, and the extent to which programming using the national language, Indonesian, will supercede ones made in Balinese.

If change is not in the control of the media, where does it reside? Perhaps in the boundaries of efficacy. It has been argued that, hybridisation and modernity apart, what has been constant in Bali is the separation of the religious centre from the political (Stuart-Fox 1991). It is possible that this separation is being challenged by television. Comparative evidence from an analysis of 'television talk' in Belize suggests that whatever the lack of power of the state to control what is beamed in via the satellites, 'television imperialism may do more to create a national culture and national consciousness . . . than 40 years of nationalist politics and 11 years of independence' (Wilk 1993: 241).

The purposeful instrumentality of the state control of media in Bali is no longer unrivalled. Since the research project started in 1990, the state monopoly of broadcasting has been challenged by deregulation. This might suggest that there have been significant changes to the relationship of power and media. However, although cable facilities which have arisen from deregulation are not state-controlled as such, they are not far from the centre of power. In 1988, President Suharto's second son Bambang Trihatmodjo set up RCTI, a private station in Jakarta; and in 1991 Suharto's eldest child, Siti Hardiyanti Rukmana, launched an educational station, Televisi Pendidikan Indonesia. Soon after, STCV, a channel broadcasting from Surabaya in East Java was established, and this can be received in Bali. In the case of Indonesia, 'deregulation' might require a special gloss.

For now, though, state interests are represented in deregulated facilities, but while the President's family controls the deregulated media, the ability of the state to ensure that audiences watch particular programmes has become more unpredictable. Increasingly, Balinese people (in the research household and, one supposes, elsewhere in Bali) watch the Surabaya station, because it shows American action films, and the traditional performance slot on the Balinese station of Indonesian State Television has become less popular. One wonders, then, for whom Gung Kak's cultural exemplars of Balineseness are being produced, apart from foreign researchers who might use the archive produced by the project. Will the external eye end up sustaining products implying identities which are quite at odds with the cultural imports consumed by the holders of those identities?[10]

Conclusions

Vickers (1996: 27) suggests that the Balinese have always had to externalise their culture for others. He does not suggest why this is the case, and whether this says something about the general nature of culture, or about the particular geo-economic position of Bali. Friedman recognises that externality is contingent on trends in western thought, 'a modernist experience of alterity with respect to the world, an alterity expressed in objectification' (1994: 77).

It is perhaps this objectification which makes for an unease in conjoining what has been labelled as traditional, ritualised and exoticised with the mundane technologies of our everyday life. World systems theory can inform and refine our understanding of sociocultural similarities (Rosaldo 1989) and put us on our guard against the essentialist bequest of structural functionalism to our concept of society and culture. But we also need to remember that these recent theories are not free of standpoints. It is vital to see the play of difference as well as the play of similarity, and to defend micro-theory against the trend for the macro. We cannot understand social transformations by fixing our gaze on television and television practices alone. To understand television in society in Bali and elsewhere, we need to understand social process in the past and the present. We are able to rub against two grains in anthropology: against extreme particularism, which too often runs the risk of essentialising otherness and producing representations which are perceived as exotic, and against extreme generalisation, which runs the risk of bringing in assumptions which deny the particularities of social process in particular places.

An anthropological contribution to the analysis of television in society therefore offers the possibility of correcting extreme tendencies to become too general or too particular, to deconstruct our own analytical presuppositions, and to strive to produce judicious ethnography and balanced images of emergent patterns of the forms of identity (social, personal, role, image, etc.) and their ongoing transformations.

Notes

1 These issues are considered in more detail in Hughes-Freeland 1998.
2 See, for example, the way in which power play in Bali is framed in terms of ritual and theatre (Geertz 1980).
3 A recent example of this stereotype is the title of a programme broadcast in Britain on 16 December 1997 on the *National Geographic* channel: *Bali: Island of Artists.*
4 DeBoer is an American scholar. Professor Dr I Made Bandem is director of Bali's prestigious State Academy of Arts, STSI, and serves as Bali's representative in the Indonesian House of Representatives in Jakarta. He is a Balinese authority on Balinese culture, yet he speaks as a Balinese with a national role and an international audience: the book is in English. It identifies performance typologies, including the sacred and the profane, developed at a seminar in the 1970s which was designed to tackle the threat of tourism to performance. Interestingly, in another work which seeks to *deconstruct* early external authorities, there is also hybridisation at work: the authors are Jensen, an American psychiatrist, and Suryani, a Balinese spirit medium with a training in American psychiatry (1992).
5 These broadcasts were made in the weekly slot then reserved for traditional performance produced by the local Balinese station of Indonesian State Television (TVRI) (Hughes-Freeland 1992).
6 Nor was there any suggestion that the play is scripted for the televised performance. This is different from Java, where actors have complained to me about the way in which the scripting of *kethoprak* plays for television is in turn altering the way live performances are produced, using scripts where before the dialogue was improvised.
7 This finding is similar to those of Abu-Lughod's research. In Egypt, villagers incorporate television into their everyday lives, and although the soap operas they watch bring added excitement to their lives, it does not displace what is already there. As such, these villagers are 'elusive targets for the cultural elite's modernising messages' (1995: 203).
8 A dramatic document about the impact of television on a community is Dennis O'Rourke's film, *Yap – How Did You Know We'd Like TV?* about the arrival of television on the Pacific island of Yap in the 1980s.
9 Shorter cremations are favoured by some because they save time, labour and money (Connor 1996).
10 Despite the political changes following President Suharto's resignation on 21 May 1988, this question remains relevant. What will happen to the Suharto family's media interests is at present uncertain.

Bibliography

Abu-Lughod, L. (1995) 'The Objects of Soap Opera: Egyptian Television and the Cultural Politics of Modernity', in D. Miller (ed.) *Worlds Apart: Modernity through the Prism of the Local*, London: Routledge, 190–210.

Aditjondro, G. (n.d.) 'Bali, Jakarta's Colony: The Domination of Jakarta-based Conglomerates in Bali's Tourism Industry and its Disastrous Social and Ecological Impact', paper to the Bali Modernity Project Wollongong Workshop, University of Wollongong, NSW, Australia, 10–11 July 1995.

Bandem, I Made and deBoer, F. E. [1981] (1995) *Balinese Dance in Transition: Kaja and Kelod*, Kuala Lumpur: Oxford University Press.

Bateson, G. and Mead, M. (1942) *Balinese Character: A Photographic Analysis*, New York: New York Academy of Sciences.

Baudrillard, J. (1988) [1970] 'Consumer Society', in M. Poster (ed.) *Jean Baudrillard: Selected Writings*, Stanford CA: Stanford University Press.

Caldarola, V. (1994) 'Embracing the Media Simulacrum', *Visual Anthropology Review*, 10, 1: 66–9.

Coast, J. (1954) *Dancing out of Bali*, London: Faber.

Cohen, A. P. (1994) *Self-Consciousness: An Alternative Anthropology of Identity*, London: Routledge.

Connor, L. (1996) 'Contestation and Transformation of Balinese Ritual: The Case of *Ngaben* Ngirit', in A. Vickers (ed.) *Being Modern in Bali: Image and Change*, Monograph 43, New Haven CT: Yale University Southeast Asian Studies, 179–211.

Covarrubias, M. (1976) [1937] *Island of Bali*, Kuala Lumpur: Oxford University Press.

deBoer, F. E. (1996) 'Two Modern Balinese Theatre Genres: *Sendratari* and *Drama Gong*', in A. Vickers (ed.) *Being Modern in Bali*, Monograph 43, New Haven CT: Yale University Southeast Asian Studies, 158–78.

De Zoete, B. and Spies, W. (1938) *Dance and Drama in Bali*, London: Faber.

Fabian, J. (1983) *Time and the Other*, New York: Columbia University Press.

Friedman, J. (1994) *Cultural Identity and Global Process*, London: Sage.

Geertz, C. (1973) *The Interpretation of Cultures*, New York: Basic Books.

——(1980) *Negara: The Theatre State in Nineteenth-Century Bali*, Princeton NJ: Princeton University Press.

Ginsburg, F. (1994a) 'Some Thoughts on Culture/Media', *Visual Anthropology Review*, 10, 1: 136–41.

——(1994b) 'Culture/Media: A (Mild) Polemic', *Anthropology Today*, 10, 2: 5–15.

Hobart, M. (1985a) 'Thinker, Thespian, Soldier, Slave: Assumptions About Human Nature in the Study of Balinese Society', in M. Hobart and R. Taylor (eds) *Context and Meaning in South East Asia*, Ithaca NY: Cornell University Press.

——(1985b) 'Anthropos Through the Looking Glass', in J. Overing (ed.) *Reason and Morality*, ASA Monograph 24, London: Tavistock.

——(1991) 'Criticizing Genres: Bakhtin in Bali', in P. Baxter and R. Fardon (eds) *Voice, Genre, Text – Anthropological Essays in Africa and Beyond*, Bulletin of the John Ryland Library, University of Manchester, 73, 3: 195–216.

——(1995) 'Engendering Disquiet: On Kinship and Gender in Bali', in W. Jahan Karim (ed.) *'Male' and 'Female' in Developing Southeast Asia*, Oxford: Berg.

Hughes-Freeland, F. (1992) 'Representation by the Other: Indonesia Cultural Documentation', in P. Crawford and D. Turton (eds) *Film as Ethnography*, Manchester: Manchester University Press.

——(1995) 'Making History: Cultural Documentation on Balinese TV', *Review of Indonesian and Malaysian Affairs*, 29, 1 & 2: 95–106.

——(1997) 'Balinese on Television: Representation and Response', in H. Morphy and M. Banks (eds) *Rethinking Visual Anthropology*, New Haven CT: Yale University Press.

——(1998) 'Introduction', in F. Hughes-Freeland (ed.) *Ritual, Performance, Media* (ASA monograph 35), London: Routledge.

Jensen, G. and Suryani, L. K. (1992) *The Balinese People*, Oxford: Oxford University Press.

McKean, P. F. (1989) 'Towards a Theoretical Analysis of Tourism: Economic Dualism and Cultural Involution in Bali', in V. L. Smith (ed.) *Hosts and Guests: The Anthropology of Tourism*, 2nd edn, Philadelphia PA: University of Pennsylvania Press.

Picard, M. (1996) 'Dance and Drama in Bali: The Making of an Indonesian Art Form', in A. Vickers (ed.) *Being Modern in Bali*, Monograph 43, New Haven CT: Yale University Southeast Asian Studies, 115–57.

Pollman, T. (1990) 'Margaret Mead's Balinese: The Fitting Symbols of the American Dream', *Indonesia*, 49: 1–35.

Reid, A. (1993) *Southeast Asia in the Age of Commerce, 1450–1680, Volume Two: Expansion and Crisis*, New Haven CT and London: Yale University Press.

Rosaldo, R. (1989) *Culture and Truth: The Remaking of Social Analysis*, Boston, MA: Beacon Press.

Rudie, I. (1994) *Visible Women in East Coast Malay Society*, Oslo: University of Oslo Press.

Schulte Nordholt, H. (1986) *Bali: Colonial Conceptions and Political Change, 1700–1940*, Rotterdam: Erasmus University, CASP.

Spitulnik, D. (1993) 'Anthropology and Mass Media', *Annual Review of Anthropology*, 22: 293–315.

Stuart-Fox, D. J. (1991) 'Pura Besakih: Temple-State Relations from Precolonial to Modern Times', in H. Geertz (ed.) *State and Society in Bali*, Leiden: KITLV Press, 11–42.

Turner, V. W. (1974) *Drama, Fields and Metaphors*, Ithaca NY: Cornell University Press.

Vickers, A. (1989) *Bali: A Paradise Created*, Singapore and Berkeley CA: Periplus.

——(ed.) (1994) *Travelling to Bali: Four Hundred Years of Journeys*, Singapore: Oxford University Press.

——(ed.) (1996) *Being Modern in Bali: Image and Change*, Monograph 43, New Haven CT: Yale University Southeast Asian Studies.

Warren, C. (1991) 'Adat and Dinas: Village and State in Contemporary Bali', in H. Geertz (ed.) *State and Society in Bali*, Leiden: KITLV Press, 213–50.

Wikan, U. (1990) *Managing Turbulent Hearts: A Balinese Formula for Living*, Chicago IL: University of Chicago Press.

Wilk, R. R. (1993) ' "It's Destroying a Whole Generation": Television and Moral Discourse in Belize', *Visual Anthropology*, 5, 3–4: 229–44.

Chapter 4

Performances of masculinity in a Maltese *festa*

Jon P. Mitchell

Every year in February, the parish of St Paul's Shipwreck in the Maltese capital city of Valletta commemorates the arrival of its patron. The commemoration takes the form of a *festa* (feast) that lasts for six days, culminating on the saint's day itself – 10 February.[1] According to local belief, St Paul was shipwrecked on Malta in AD 60, converting the local people and setting in motion the continuous tradition of Maltese Catholicism. This centrality of St Paul in the historical account of the Maltese people means that he is not only the local patron of St Paul's parish, but also the national patron saint. His commemoration, known as *San Pawl*, is likewise both local and national. The saint's day is a national holiday, and a church day of obligation – all Maltese are obliged to hear mass. The *pontifikal* (pontifical mass) on *festa* day is said by the Archbishop of Malta and attended by important political figures – the President and leaders of the Nationalist Party.[2] In 1993, the *pontifikal* was broadcast live on national television for the first time. Since then, people who are unable to attend the mass have also been allowed to participate in the national celebration.

As a public ritual broadcast on national media, involving prominent members of state and religious institutions, *San Pawl* can be seen as a representation of national identity, the power of the state and the hegemony of the Catholic church. Such an interpretation would echo those of Binns (1979, 1980) and Lane (1981) on the ritual repertoire of the Soviet Union, and Cohn (1983) on that of the British colonists in India. In these cases, ritual is both representation of power and appeal to collective identity. This quasi-Durkheimian approach to ritual has had something of a resurgence in recent years, with ethnographers attempting to understand the social significance of public ritual, or spectacle, and its place in the construction and elaboration of collective identity (Geertz 1973; Foucault 1977; Kapferer 1988; Handelman

1990; Boissevain 1992). Yet alongside this concern with the collective, there has also been a growing interest in the significance of public ritual in the construction and elaboration of personal – particularly gender – identities. Again, this has a venerable anthropological heritage, in the work of Turner, for whom the collective was constructed through the production of the person (1969). This is most clear in the analysis of initiation rituals, which are specifically concerned with the production of persons, and subjecting the individual to the social requirements of the person. More recent writers have extended this work, focusing on the extent to which initiation produces gendered persons (Herdt 1982, 1987; Godelier 1986; Brock-Due *et al.* 1993; Lutkehaus and Roscoe 1995).

It has become received wisdom that gender identities are not intrinsic to men and women, but are socially constructed (Ortner 1974; Moore 1988; Lacqueur 1990). Studies of initiation focus on the extent to which this construction takes place through ritual. Initiation rituals often involve not only the inculcation or ascription of gender identities, but also their literal incorporation, through bodily inscriptions such as circumcision, scarification or body-piercing. These inscriptions have been seen as indices or representations of gender categories. Yet the constructive process is not merely symbolic, apparent at the level of cultural categories inscribed on the body. It is also performative, or substantively incorporated into the body (Butler 1990, Morris 1995). Connell (1995) has recently criticised purely social constructionist theories of gender. He suggests that rather than seeing the human organism as *tabula rasa* upon which gender categories are inscribed, the body interacts with this inscription process, to perform a constructive 'body agency' which sees gender emerging from a dialectic of culture-cognitive and body-cognitive production. In other words, rather than simply being inscribed on the body, the categories of gender are actually embodied. This approach tallies with Csordas' (1990) model of an 'embodiment paradigm', and is adopted here. It parallels research in ritual studies, where ritual is conceived of as simultaneously a social and a bodily practice (Bell 1992; Parkin 1992; Humphrey and Laidlaw 1994).

This chapter focuses on the significance of the *San Pawl* ritual for the people actively participating in its performance, particularly the group of men who are chosen to carry the monumental statue of St Paul during the procession on 10 February. I argue that carrying the statue is related to gender, and the process of masculinity. I view statue-carrying as a bodily practice which involves both the social categories of masculinity and their incorporation in the male bodies which perform the act. Through carrying the statue, men produce themselves as a particular category of men – *reffiegha* (statue-carriers) – who command a certain prestige in the local community because of their performative competence in statue-carrying. This competence is inscribed on the physical body of the statue-carrier, in the form of a large callus on the shoulders – known as *hobza*, or 'bread bun' – which provides a focus for their competence, and for their capacity to perform a bodily act in a public arena.

From the perspective of initiation, such ritual processes could be seen as the means by which gender is produced. In this case, lifting a statue and participating in the *festa* creates a category of man who is identifiable by the callus on his shoulder. But gender is not only produced through the relatively extraordinary or one-off performances. It is also constituted through performance in everyday contexts through the adoption of particular, gendered modes of comportment, body hexis or *habitus* (Bourdieu 1990). As Butler puts it, gender is 'always a doing' – an active performance that constitutes gendered being (1990: 25). The everyday performances of social life are every bit as important – perhaps even more so – as those associated with the one-off, spectacular ritual occasions of initiation or *festa* (Morris 1995: 576). Where ethnographers focus exclusively on the spectacular, they do so at the cost of the everyday (de Certeau 1984).

The ethnography of *festa* provides an important point of mediation between these two extremes of gendered performance: the extraordinary and the everyday. On the one hand, it resembles initiation in that it produces a type of man through incorporative practice. On the other hand, it differs from initiation in that it is repeated annually by the same men. Moreover, it is entirely dependent on the more mundane everyday performances associated more broadly with masculinity. Unlike other intitiation rituals or rites of passage, statue-carrying in the *festa* is not open to all. Rather, the 'initiands' must first show their competence as men in an everyday context, before they are chosen to be *reffiegha*. Only those already regarded as being 'good men' are considered for the position of *reffiegh*. In *festa*, therefore, the ritual and the everyday lie in a dialectical relationship whereby everyday performances determine who is suitable to perform ritually, and ritual performances determine what type of man is performing in the everyday.

As suggested by Lindisfarne (1994) and Connell (1995), there is no single context in which gender is performed and constructed. It therefore follows that there is no single masculinity. Rather, a range of masculinities exist in any one social context. In dealing with the variations in masculinity it has been most common to examine the various types of subordinate or resistant masculinities – associated particularly with homosexuality, cross-dressing and drag performance (Morris 1995). However, there is also variation within the 'hegemonic masculinity' in relation to which these divergent masculinities are constructed. I treat the category *reffiegha* as a particular, variant manifestation of Maltese hegemonic masculinity (Vale de Almeida 1996). In order to understand what this hegemonic masculinity constitutes, it is first necessary to examine gender and gender studies in the Mediterranean region as a whole.

Gender and anthropology in the Mediterranean

The anthropology of gender in the Mediterranean has been dominated by the paradigmatic identification of an 'honour and shame' moral code that has been seen as a defining feature of the region (Peristiany 1965; Pitt-Rivers 1977; Gilmore 1987). The honour/shame syndrome relates to the household, and in particular the gendered division of social space into public and private domains (Rosaldo 1974; Reiter 1975; Hirschon 1981). According to this paradigm, the honour of a household is linked to the reputation of the women who live there (Pitt-Rivers 1961; Campbell 1964). Their reputation is sealed by the public display of shame, as manifest in a reticence towards appearing in public places. Shame is therefore connected to women's association with the domestic domain of the house itself. Honour, on the other hand, is connected to men's association with the public domain outside the house. What emerges is a picture of Mediterranean society composed of secluded, female-oriented households linked together by the social ties created by men in the public domain.

This view of Mediterranean society has recently been criticised for presenting a stereotype of the Mediterranean that serves to distance the Mediterranean from Northern Europe and North America – a kind of 'Mediterraneanism' akin to Said's Orientalism (Said 1978; Herzfeld 1984, 1987; Pina-Cabral 1989). This over-generalises the unity of the Mediterranean and thereby ignores the range of different gender ideologies that coexist within that setting, encouraging the portayal of only an 'official' version of Mediterranean gender ideology that sustains the image of the hegemonic male (Goddard 1987; Loizos and

Papataxiarchis 1991; Lindisfarne 1994). These critiques have two main consequences. First, they open up space for recognising and analysing the differences between the hegemonic models of gender and its daily practice. This has particularly influenced ethnographers of women in the Mediterranean, who have repeatedly demonstrated women's substantive public roles, in contrast to their apparent privatisation. Second, they suggest the hegemonic model of gender and its modes of reproduction as itself an object of study. In this context, attention has been drawn to the importance of everyday performance in the production of gender (Herzfeld 1985; Cowan 1991).

Practice against hegemony – hegemony through performance

By suggesting that Mediterranean society is built up by active men in a public, cultural domain, who create links between the domestic, natural domain of the household (Harris 1981) – itself characterised by passive women – anthropologists have underestimated the active role of women in creating Mediterranean social structures. Dubisch has argued that through their everyday 'kin-work', women in rural Greece produce Greek society. By 'kin-work' she means the daily 'tasks that sustain family networks' (Dubisch 1991: 38). These tasks are organised around the central unit of Greek kinship – the mother–daughter relationship. She proposes a 'reconsideration' of the anthropology of Greece, to take account of women's active role and thereby acknowledge the practice of daily life that lies behind the hegemonic model of gender. One might pursue this approach when examining other Mediterranean contexts, not least Malta.

Like Greece, Malta is strongly uxorilateral (Mizzi 1981; Sant Cassia 1993). Social life is organised around the concept of the household. But the household is not unequivocally associated with women. Rather, the household is conceived of as a unit of gender complementarity, centred on a single married couple. Ideally, a household should occupy a single house, which is both a dwelling place and a symbolic representation of the family.

The household is organised around the categories *gewwa* and *barra* (inside and outside). These, in turn, relate to categories of person. Those *ta'gewwa* (of the inside) are either members of the household, close kin from outside the household, or particularly friendly neighbours. At a practical level, they are people who can turn up uninvited, and be welcomed into the house. These are usually matrilateral kin.

The term *ta'barra* (of the outside) is seldom used in this context, but logically applies to everybody else.

Knowledge of relations outside the household varies according to gender. Both men and women normally generalise kin more distant than first cousins as *kugini* (cousins). But whereas women generally know the details of this relatedness, men have a vaguer idea. As well as bearing the knowledge of relatedness, women also organise these social links, and make sure that the family ties are maintained. As well as this 'kin-work' and 'neighbourhood-work', women are also largely responsible for maintaining links with the dead. This is a common feature of Mediterranean societies, and ensures that trips to church perform a double function (Danforth 1982; Davis 1984; Dubisch 1995). These activities are crucial for the production and maintenance of Maltese society, and take place outside the house, through daily trips to grocery shops, churches and public meetings. For although household 'insiders' are usually matrilateral kin, this does not mean to say that women are confined to the household. Neither does it mean that theirs is a passive role in Maltese society. Rather, they actively participate in a public life, and through this create social ties and social structure. In the process, however, they also constitute themselves as women. This process, although performative, can reproduce the hegemonic model of ideal femininity. Public performances therefore reinforce the notion that women's roles are primarily domestic.

Indeed, within the household women play a critical role. They are generally responsible for the day-to-day maintenance of the household, involving not only cooking, cleaning and childcare, but also frequently administering the household budget. They must therefore balance their participation in the public worlds of kinship and society, with sufficient commitment and attention to the domestic domain. Again, their everyday performances go towards producing themselves as women. Through cooking, for example, women demonstrate their competence in budgeting, provisioning and preparing for the house-hold – a practical manifestation or performance of the balance between inside and outside that is needed to be a successful woman (see also Goddard 1996: 205–13).

As well as this everyday production of female identity, women also perform in extraordinary contexts. These are most commonly associated with religious pilgrimages such as Our Lady of Sorrows (*Id-Duluri*), which draws thousands – mainly women – to Valletta to walk barefoot behind the statue of Our Lady on the Friday before Good Friday. This is a manifestation on the scale of St Paul's *festa*, but

with an entirely different atmosphere. Whereas *San Pawl* is characterised by sociability and revelry, *Id-Duluri* is much more solemn and
subdued. The performances are also different. Whereas the procession
of St Paul involves a public manifestation by men of their abilities and
competencies as *reffiegħa*, the pilgrimage of Our Lady involves
women's personal and intimate demonstration of faith and devotion.
Such performances have their own distinct poetics, which link the
suffering of Our Lady to the hegemonic model of the woman as a
long-suffering, faithful servant to family and society (Dubisch 1995:
212–28; Goddard 1996: 183–203).

Women have a central position in the Maltese world. Their
authority over the household and pivotal role in creating extra-
household ties means that men are often alienated from this central
institution. It is common, for example, for women to send their
husbands out of the house because they are 'getting in the way'. For
men to be out of the household too much, however, is equally
censured. Men, like women, should ideally strike a balance between
being inside and being outside.

As in other Mediterranean contexts, the centrality of women in the
household and their active role in the creation of social ties is balanced
by men's prestige in a public domain (Pina-Cabral 1986; Papataxiarchis
1988). Thus although both men and women perform in public
settings, these performances differ. Whilst women are expected to meet
up during shopping trips or 'coffee mornings', men participate in
public debate by regularly attending political meetings, engaging in
gossip at local bars or clubs, and organising events such as the *festa*.

The differences between male and female competencies and performances are openly acknowledged in everyday discourse. The balance
required between activities inside and outside the house, in both men's
and women's lives, creates a tension of expectations manifest in the
comments of the different genders about each other. They take the
form of a kind of mutual trivialisation between men and women, which
has the effect of simultaneously denying and acknowledging the legitimacy of each other's gender identity. On the one hand, when talking
of women, men will trivialise their social role, regarding their conversations as irrelevant *tlablib* (talkativeness, chit-chat). They will deny the
importance of 'coffee mornings' and other meetings, and tease women
about the long hours spent talking to neighbours in the local grocery
shops. On the other hand, men will acknowledge women's social role,
and even fear it. Their social relations are seen as opportunities for the
dangerous spread of information or intrigue by a *caccaruna* (gossip).

The fear of this social role is manifest in men's hyperbolic statements that they should lock their wives indoors before going to work, and more distressingly in high levels of domestic violence.[3] When talking of men, women will similarly trivialise their role in the public domain. In particular, their daily, weekly obsession with football and *festa* are ridiculed. The public pursuit of status through activities such as statue-carrying is derided as pointless. But on the other hand, women encourage their husbands to participate in such games, and regard the public – and predominantly male – pursuits of politics and *festa* as important. Without them the performance of masculinity is incomplete, and men – particularly young men – are encouraged by mothers, wives and sisters to participate.

Fieldwork in Malta

I spent nine of my twenty-two months of fieldwork living with a Maltese family, which is unusual for a young male anthropologist in the Mediterranean. This gave me first-hand knowledge of Maltese domestic life, and a position from which to observe the everyday performances of masculinity and femininity. But as is common to much Mediterranean ethnography by men, my fieldwork mainly centred on male social groups in a public domain (see Brandes 1980; Herzfeld 1985). The focus on male sociality was partly dictated by the subject of my research – the administration and performance of *San Pawl* is undertaken predominantly by men. However, it was also shaped by local Maltese perceptions of my gender identity, and prescriptions of appropriate behaviour. As Brandes pointed out with regard to fieldwork in Andalucia, 'gender identity, like . . . age, marital status, and personality, will always in some way intervene [in research]' (Brandes 1992: 38). As a young man, I was encouraged by men and women to participate as much as possible in male sociability outside the house. I was therefore introduced to the areas of male sociability, where masculinity is produced through the everyday practice of social life – in particular, a small local bar known as *Ghand Lawrenz* ('Lawrence's Place', literally 'at the home of Lawrence'). In this context, masculinity is not so much performance as performativity – a manifestation of skilled male practice.

The proper name of *Ghand Lawrenz* is *San Paolo Naufragio* (St Paul's Shipwreck) which reveals its significance for those interested in the *festa* of *San Pawl*. Conversation in the bar revolves around *festa* and the activity of statue-carrying. *San Pawl* is not the only context in which statues are carried. They are also carried during the Good Friday procession that is organised from the nearby Franciscan church. During that procession, seven statues move around the city, accompanied by people dressed in elaborate pageant costumes. However, *San Pawl* is the most important statue carried during the year, and it is carrying the statue of St Paul that many of the younger denizens of *Ghand Lawrenz* aspire to.

The bar is the unofficial clubhouse of the *Pawlini* (Paulites). The term *Pawlini* broadly denotes supporters of *San Pawl*, be they locals to the parish or outsiders. More specifically, however, it marked out members of the organisation that was set up in the early 1970s to oversee the administration of the *festa*, the *Ghaqda tal-Pawlini* (Association of *Pawlini*). More specifically still, it denoted the group of men who were at the centre of the *Ghaqda*, who bore the greatest responsibility for, and contributed the most work to the *festa*.

Although not limited to men, the *Ghaqda tal-Pawlini* is dominated by them. The central committee of twenty-two has only one woman member, and she is a delegate from the commission for women, set up in 1991. Were it not for this executive delegation, there would probably be no woman on the committee. The Annual General Meetings at which the committee are elected are nearly all-male affairs, and the day-to-day running of the organisation is carried out primarily by men. Moreover, it is conducted *Ghand Lawrenz*, which makes it problematic for women to participate, because women tend to avoid going to bars.

The *festa*

Organising the *festa* involves a year-long process of fundraising and maintaining the elaborate street decorations. In the few months before the *festa*, the police must be contacted and licences obtained, brass bands booked, and fireworks purchased. In the final few weeks, large numbers of unpaid labourers must be mobilised to decorate the streets and church. The group of men who are to carry the statue must also be chosen. These are the men who will have both the honour and the responsibility of making sure the most important part of the *festa* – the procession of St Paul's statue – is done well.

Structurally, all *festi* are similar. They comprise five or six days of celebration, which involves solemn prayer-meetings and sung masses, lengthy sermons and blessings, lively brass band marches and fireworks displays. A categorical distinction is made between festivities occurring inside the church and administered by the clergy (*festi ta'gewwa*) and those which take place outside the church and are administered by the laity (*festi ta'barra*). These latter activities are the primary responsibility of the *Ghaqda tal-Pawlini*.

Throughout the six days of *festa* the inside and outside festivities run parallel, and are scheduled so that as inside festivities end, outside events begin. For example, on the three days preceding *festa* eve (9 February) a series of masses known as *it-tridu* is held. This includes a long sermon given over the three days by a visiting priest. In it, the priest teaches about important parts of the saint's life. In the case of St Paul, the *tridu* focuses on the contribution he made to Maltese history and culture. As each *tridu* draws to a close, a band march is timed to begin outside the church, so that people who have attended the inside festivity can also participate in the outside event. Inside and outside festivities are complementary, and differ in atmosphere. The relative solemnity of events inside the church contrasts with the often drunken and enthusiastic *briju* (brio, merrymaking) of those outside. The two domains are brought together at the climax of the *festa* on 10 February itself.

Festa day is characterised by three events, the first involving the inside *festa*, the second the outside *festa*, and the third bringing the two together. The first event is the lengthy *pontifikal* (pontifical mass) said by the Archbishop. This is the most important part of the inside *festa*. The second is timed to begin at the end of the *pontifikal*. It is the popular *marc tas-siegha* (one o'clock march) that is the climax of the outside festivities. It is the most raucous of the band marches. The streets of Valletta swell with approximately 10,000 revellers. In front of the band large groups of young men congregate, getting progressively more drunk as the march proceeds. The route of the march takes this group round the streets of Valletta and back to St Paul's Church in time to meet the beginning of the main procession.

The main procession is the pinnacle of the *festa*, and the most important event of the year for the *Pawlini*. As it prepares to leave the church, large crowds gather outside the front door of the church. The band, which is especially chosen for its ability to play rousing marches, waits to the side. The procession is led by the Valletta religious confraternities,[4] who wear long white smocks and carry their standards. After them come representatives of the religious orders that have communities in Valletta – including the Augustinians, Carmelites, Dominicans and Franciscans. Next are the members of the Canonic Chapter of St Paul's Shipwreck itself, who accompany the holy relic of St Paul,[5] and the Archpriest who carries the host. Behind them is the statue. As it leaves the church a huge volley of airborne fireworks is set off from a nearby garden, and firecrackers explode on the church roof. After coming down the six steps out of the church, the statue is taken on its route.

Valletta was built by the Knights of St John in 1565, using a grid system that marked it as an epitome of what Mumford describes as the ceremonially oriented baroque city (1970: 97). The grid design was superimposed on the hunch-backed Xiberras peninsula, which means that many of the streets have steep slopes. Some had to be stepped to prevent accidents. St Paul's Shipwreck Church lies in a hollow on St Paul's Street.

The route of the procession goes from the church and up a gentle slope, before cutting across to Republic Street, Valletta's main thoroughfare. After climbing further, the procession stops outside St John's Co-Cathedral[6] where a large crowd says prayers and sings the hymn of St Paul. The procession then turns once more, up Market Street, and then back onto St Paul's Street, for the steep descent back to the church.

The procession is accompanied by crowds. The streets are packed with people who sing along with the lively band marches. At every corner the procession stops and the statue is turned round to 'look' down the streets through which it will not be passing. This demonstrates the patronage of St Paul over his parish. As with similar occasions in other Mediterranean contexts, the importance of the *festa* is that it ensures the continued influence of the saint over his congregation (see Kertzer 1980; Pina-Cabral 1986).

The statue and the *reffiegha*

The statue of St Paul was carved from wood by Melchiorre Gafà (1635–67), an associate of Bernini and exponent of the Baroque. Commissioned by the Maltese aristocratic family Testaferrata, it was donated by them to the church (Ciarlò 1995: 42). It is regarded as an important part of the national patrimony (*il-patrimonju nazzjonali*), as a physical embodiment of the Maltese conversion.

It is more than a mere representation. For most of the year the statue is kept in a large niche in the church, behind a glass panel with a small offerings box in front. For the six days of *festa* it is taken out of its niche and kept on trestles in the main body of the church. The space in front of him is decorated with flowers and candles, and becomes a space where men and women congregate, to chat, pray or simply sit and stare in wonder at the presence of *L-Apostlu ta'Malta*, 'The Apostle of Malta'. Here, people can physically engage with the saint, walking around him and touching him. The statue becomes animated, an embodiment of the saint himself to whom one can talk directly, rather than simply offering a donation. When the statue is here, people avoid turning their back on him, and when they do, will apologise: 'Sorry, Pawlu'. These are days when special prayers can be offered to the saint; the possibility of direct physical engagement standing also for a more direct spiritual engagement that is assumed to increase the possibility of intercession.

A number of social theorists have argued that physical engagements with an artefact such as a statue shape thought in significant ways. Spatial cognition is of primary importance in the learning of social categories and the process of belief (see Bourdieu 1990; Toren 1990; Csordas 1994; Mitchell 1997). The cognitive significance of being able to encounter the statue in space, in close proximity, is clearly not lost on Maltese parents. Children, particularly boys, are taken to visit the saint throughout the year, but especially during this period of the *festa*, when the statue can be viewed from all angles. One parent explained to me:

> This is the nicest time to take your children to see Paul. This way they can really understand.

The fact that the statue is an embodiment of the saint, rather than simply a representation, is significant for the men who carry it. The act of carrying means an important physical engagement with not only a statue, but also a saint.

The statue is incredibly heavy, and during the procession it is carried on the shoulders by a team of twelve men known as the *reffiegha* (statue-carriers). For carrying, the statue is bolted onto a large rectangular pallet known as a *bradella*. The *bradella* has shafts running from front to back, through which large batons, *bsaten* (*batsun sing.*) are passed. It is by means of these that the statue is carried. They are evenly spaced so as to allow the *reffiegha* room to manoeuvre, and they protrude some three or four feet at front and back. They are held in place and adjusted with wooden chocks, which counteract the differences in height between different *reffiegha*. A large wooden block is bolted onto the *bastun* when one of them is particularly short.

Only eight men carry the statue at any one time. The remaining four walk alongside the statue, carrying ornate decorated forks (*forcina*) on which the statue is supported when it stops. The statue is carried on the shoulder, ideally resting on the bone that protrudes from the top of the spine. The *reffiegħ* should stand upright, with his thumbs hooked into the rope belt that holds in the roomy white gown worn for the occasion. As he walks, he should sway from side to side, moving steadily along the street so that the statue itself appears to be walking.

Swaying at will depends on being sufficiently strong to maintain control of the statue. The ability to do this is an important criterion for the choice of *reffiegħa*, but given the weight of the statue, it is not easy to find men who can be relied upon to competently perform the act. Those who are chosen are respected for this strength and competence.

Performative competence

Not all men are, or aspire to being *reffiegħa*. In general, it is a practice associated with the stratum of society known as either 'low' (*baxx*), or 'the people' (*il-poplu*) in opposition to 'polite society' (*il-pulit*). As such, it is a practice that produces prestige mainly within a particular status group. The *reffiegħa* I knew in Valletta were predominantly drawn from unskilled or semi-skilled employment categories with minimal education (to ages fourteen or sixteen). People of higher status tend to have a fairly ambivalent attitude towards *festa* and the practices of the *reffiegħa*. Although mainly limited to *il-poplu*, statue-carrying is nevertheless widespread throughout Malta. Each of the country's sixty-five parishes has at least one *festa* every year, at which a statue is carried, and *reffiegħa* are needed.

The ability to become a *reffiegħ* depends on the ascription or achievement of masculinity in other, everyday contexts. Becoming a *reffiegħ* is dependent on the daily performances required to 'be a man'. These involve: adopting the appropriate male bodily postures of uprightness and independence – standing with shoulders pushed back and stomach pushed out in relaxed but authoritative manner; developing a firm handshake augmented by a grasp of the upper arm, and a full 'gestural vocabulary' with which to illustrate an argument (Connerton 1989: 80); being talkative with a good sense of humour – particularly praised is the creative use of swear words and double-entendres; developing a repertoire of retorts or responses to real and apparent slights, which can be mobilised quickly when required; displaying generosity, reliability and trustworthiness; and ultimately being both heterosexual and a father (Mitchell 1996). This rather hastily presented list of attributes constitutes a basic lexicon of Maltese hegemonic masculinity, and successful performance of this *habitus* is necessary to become a *reffiegh*.

Becoming a *reffiegh* is partly hereditary. Many *reffiegha* are the sons or nephews of previous ones. The links across generations are reinforced by *Pawlini* who, during the months and weeks leading up to *San Pawl* spend their time *ghand Lawrenz* discussing past *festi*. It is common for them to bring photograph albums from previous years, which they can use to identify characters from the past and make judgements about these veterans' statue-carrying abilities. Particularly competent men are pointed out by identifying their stature during the procession. If in the photographs they stand upright with hand in belt, their abilities are praised: this is the approved aesthetic. If, on the other hand, their back is bent, criticisms will emerge. Attention will be drawn to their being *mghaweg* (crooked) or *imkisser* (broken).

This evaluation on the basis of pictorial media is extended not only to the distant past but also to the more recent. The prevalence of camcorders means that the procession is captured on videotape every year. The tapes are played over and over again in the small bar, and a critical commentary on statue-carrying competency is offered by all those present. When *reffiegha* are there, they draw attention to their own abilities, and others tease them about the strained expressions on their faces, or their slight stumbles. Links are made between the present *reffiegha* and the past. Men who have *reffiegh* predecessors are compared to them, normally favourably.

It is generally assumed that a man whose father or uncle was a good *reffiegh* will also be a good one. This is partly related to physical stature. Given the weight of the statue, some men are never going to be strong enough to carry St Paul. There is therefore a degree of genetic determinism in the production of *reffiegha* for *San Pawl*. But strength is not the only thing that is needed to be a good *reffiegh*. In the words of the *Pawlini*, a *reffiegh* must be *ragel sew* (a good man). The category *ragel sew* is an evaluative, moral category, which relates to trustworthiness and reputation for reliability, connectedness in the public domain and strength of religious belief. These are important features of masculinity, which are both a prerequisite for, and produced through, becoming *reffiegha*. I shall deal with each in turn.

First, being *ragel sew* relates to reliability and trustworthiness. The statue is the property of the church, and every year those chosen by the *Ghaqda tal-Pawlini* to carry it around the parish are asked to sign a contract which makes the *Ghaqda* responsible for any damage. This is a big responsibility, given the weight of the statue and the number of hills up which it must be carried. The only way to succeed in the task is through proper teamwork, with everybody taking their share of the burden. This is referred to as 'taking your piece' (*tiehdu l-piece*). When people do not 'take their piece' it is soon made public knowledge. Word will go round that the man in question was not pulling his weight, and this jeopardises his chance of selection in subsequent years.

The miscreant shirker is referred to through metaphors of sexuality. He who shirks his responsibility and is not a good team *reffiegh* is referred to as *pufta* (homosexual) or *haxxej* (fucker). *Pufta* is a category that refers strictly speaking to transvestites, of whom there are a few in Valletta. They are acknowledged as being men, but a different kind of man from those who carry statues. Some regard them as 'mad' (*imgienen*), others as 'poor things' (*imsieken*). Either way, they are regarded as divergent from the heterosexual norm. *Haxxej* is similarly linked to homosexuality, and is the correlate of another commonly used vulgar term *hudu f'sormok* ('take it in the arse'). Stanley Brandes has argued that a similar phrase in Andalucia implies the feminisation of the recipient of the insult (Brandes 1981). I would disagree with this interpretation, arguing rather that it implies homosexualisation. The normative or hegemonic model of masculinity in Malta is not only related to images of femininity, but also to images of homosexuality and divergent masculinities. Both *pufta* and *haxxej*, therefore, imply a homosexualisation that, although acknowledging variant masculinities, nevertheless stresses the importance of heterosexuality in the production of the *ragel sew*.

The importance of heterosexuality can be linked to the reproductive role of men. If it is important for men to balance their performances in the public domain with presence in the domestic, then one of their major domestic roles is fatherhood. Fatherhood is clearly linked to masculinity, so being homosexual takes away the primary context in which men produce themselves as men. That inadequate performance as a *reffiegh* leads to a man's homosexualisation reveals the significance of statue-carrying in the process of masculinity. If a man is a good *reffiegh*, then *ipso facto* he cannot be thought of as homosexual.

The kind of reliability that avoids homosexual slurs is to a certain extent regarded as hereditary. Men who have reliable fathers or uncles are themselves regarded as reliable and trustworthy – this is partly because of the belief that a miscreant son or nephew will be sanctioned by a good father or uncle.

Second, a *ragel sew* is thought of as having the related characteristic of good connections. This is once more linked to heredity in that one of the good connections necessary is with one's immediate familial antecedents. The links of one's father or uncles to some extent determine the links one develops, such that connectedness is hereditary.

Carrying the statue is a demonstration of connectedness, because in order to be chosen as a *reffiegh*, a man must be well connected. Although there are physical limits to who is able to carry St Paul, there is a great deal of competition for selection. Many men aspire to becoming *reffiegha*, and the choice ultimately lies with the *Ghaqda tal-Pawlini*. Having connections within the *Ghaqda*, then, is important if one is to become a *reffiegh*.

For example, soon before the *festa* of 1993, one of the established *reffiegha* pulled out due to ill health. There was an immediate search for a replacement, and many men came forward. The man finally chosen was very well connected within the *Pawlini*. His father had been a good and reliable *reffiegh* during the 1960s, and his cousin was currently responsible for choosing who carried the statue. Although he had only recently returned to Malta after five years in Australia, these connections were sufficiently strong to give him a place in the final team.

He described to me his feelings on this, his first attempt at carrying St Paul, linking these personal experiences to the public context of community. While in Australia, he had performed as a *reffiegh* in the Melbourne *San Pawl*:

> It's not that they didn't have *festi* in Australia. We always celebrated *San Pawl*, and there was even a procession. But it wasn't the same. The statue wasn't very big, and there weren't many people there. In any case, there's only one St Paul.

The fact of carrying the statue by Gafà, then, is of major significance. As argued above, this statue is an embodiment, rather than mere representation, of the saint. But the importance of performing in *San Pawl*, Valletta, was also related to community:

> It makes you feel proud because you can bring everybody together. *San Pawl* brings people together. That's good, especially nowadays.

This relates to the observations of Boissevain (1992) that local festivities are becoming increasingly important in the increasingly globalised modern world. If this is the case, then responsibility for carrying the statue and making sure that the *festa* is performed properly, confers on the *reffiegħa* the status of people who bring the local community together in the face of fragmentation. In the context of *San Pawl*, however, the community that is drawn together is not merely local, it is also national. As stated above, the pontifical mass is broadcast on national television, but the procession is also covered on the national news. Amateur videos circulate in the months following the *festa* and are watched in both Valletta bars and homes throughout the country. *San Pawl* is incorporative, both locally and nationally. This media presence mirrors similar developments in the Rocio pilgrimage of southern Spain, although in that context the impact of media on the ritual itself is much more developed (Crain 1997).

Finally, being *raġel sew* confers strength of religious belief. In order to be *Pawlini*, people must demonstrate, first, their faith in the Catholic church, and second, their commitment to the teaching of St Paul. These are assured by an appropriate upbringing, so the religious implications of being *raġel sew* are linked to the piety of one's antecedents. If a man has a father or uncle who was sufficiently religious to become a *reffiegħ*, then the chances are he will be as well.

There is assumed to be a religious element in the practice of statue-carrying itself. Many people described it as a kind of penance, or *werda*. The physical and symbolic subjection of the body to the trauma of being underneath the heavy statue is a literal and figurative subjection of the person to the power of the saint (see Scarry 1985). The somatic response, or physiological symptoms of this trauma produce a kind of euphoria that *reffiegħa* find difficult to describe. The feeling is *tal-ostja* ('of the host' – a rather blasphemous but common phrase for 'amazing'). One man described the feeling as follows:

> It's incredible, the feeling that you get. I remember the first time I did it. It was like the biggest 'high' you could possibly get. You get taken over by it – it's amazing. Like [St] Paul is with you.

The man used the English word 'high' to describe his experience. He had been a drug user prior to becoming a *reffiegħ* and had used his experience of statue-carrying to help rehabilitate himself. He had got the opportunity because his father was a good and reliable *reffiegħ*, and a well-known figure in the local community.

The importance of the 'high' is that it relates the social significance of *San Pawl*, as a communal celebration which brings together both local and national communities, to the personal and bodily experience of physical engagement with the saint himself. The status of the *reffiegha*, therefore, is not only socially ascribed, but also experienced at a bodily level.

Bodily experience – bodily inscription

This experience of proximity to St Paul – this bodily engagement with the local and national patron – is inscribed on the bodies of established *reffiegha*. Men who have performed the honour have permanent, large calluses on their shoulders, as inscriptions of their experience carrying the saint. They are proud of these calluses, known as *hobza* (bread buns) because they are similar in size and shape to a traditional Maltese bread. They are displayed to the awe of young children, and with pride to the visiting ethnographer. It is a physical inscription of their capabilities, their ability to handle the statue of St Paul, and a trace of their physical engagement with him.

These bodily inscriptions perform the same role as that identified by Peteet in the traces of violence on men's bodies in Palestine (1994). There, being beaten and physically scarred becomes a kind of rite of passage for which the bodily traces become inscriptions of masculinity. The same could be said of the individual *reffiegh*'s *hobza*. Although achieved in less violent circumstances, the *hobza* is also a bodily inscription of masculinity, as it constitutes a physical trace of carrying the statue of St Paul.

Men are proud of their *hobza*. One man described to me with horror how he had been to the doctor for a check-up, and the doctor had suggested he had the large callus surgically removed. It was not only that doing so would make future statue-carrying uncomfortable. He also pointed out that it would be taking away a significant symbol of his identity. 'It's part of me', he said, 'I wouldn't let anybody take it away'. This suggests that the *hobza* is more than a mere inscription of discomfort and physical trauma. Rather, it is an incorporation or embodiment of not only the experience of carrying St Paul, but also the status that doing so produces. It serves as a focus for their status and is the object of admiration by younger men.

In the bar *Ghand Lawrenz*, men are very tactile. It is common for men to sit holding hands, with a hand on each other's knee or round the shoulders. It is also common for them to touch each other in acknowledgement of masculinity – either in jest or in admiration. Particular foci of this kind of touching are the penis, the belly and the *hobza*. The penis is often grabbed as a joking challenge. Men attempt to elicit a response in the form of either mock physical violence, or more entertainingly, a witty riposte.[7] The belly is gently patted either by a man himself or another, to demonstrate the man's comfort and lack of anxiety. A healthily sized belly is considered a sign of happiness, and particularly of being settled in a comfortable domestic relationship. The *hobza* is revealed by *reffiegha* to younger men who aspire to carry the statue. They often grab it as they walk past a seated *reffiegha*, and caress it with wonder at its size and consistency. It is a focus of their aspirations – something to be achieved in the future. To this extent, it is the embodiment of a particular variant of masculinity, to which the younger men aspire.

Statue-carrying and the aspirations of the young

Becoming a *reffiegh* for *San Pawl* fits into a recognisable *festa* career, or developmental process. It is the culmination of aspirations which start at an early age. Children and young men spend time practising, or *training* to become *reffiegha* in their spare time.

During my fieldwork, one set of twins, aged thirteen in 1994, would practise their technique using the large wooden trestles used to support the Good Friday statues during the year. To their delight, and that of their father, they chose to carry on different shoulders. This would make them a perfect complementary pair when they graduated to the real thing. They could each occupy a position at the front corner, on the inside of their *bastun*, to ensure absolute symmetry. Carrying with the head on the outside is considered unsightly, but a lack of left-shouldered *reffiegha* sometimes means it is necessary.

The twins would take their places at either end of a trestle, and then invite one of the adult men to hang from the centre. With the time-honoured signal, '*fuq*' (up), they would lift, and begin their swaying progress along the church corridor. When they reached the end, another call would come, '*forcina*', and the trestle would be lowered. Here, the boys were explicitly drawing on the terminology of the procession in order to add a certain atmosphere to their *training*, rather as in other circumstances they would add commentary to their football games.

This form of *training* is common. Experienced *reffiegha* told me that they also trained when they were younger. They would take a large pole and suspend from it two oil drums filled with water. Then they would parade up and down the street. At first people thought they were mad, but then when they became *reffiegha* they were filled with admiration: it had been worth it.

When they get older, boys start to participate in the Good Friday procession, carrying the lighter statues associated with that event. They also take a 'piece' during the *San Pawl* procession. On the last leg of the procession, as the statue comes down the steep hill of St Paul's Street and towards the church, the main group of *reffiegha* leave the statue in the charge of a couple of ex-*reffiegha*. This is the opportunity for young men from the parish to have a go at carrying the statue, and establish their credentials as potential *reffiegha*. The men crowd round the statue, jostling for positions on the *bsaten*. Sometimes more than one man occupies a position on the same *bastun*, and this can lead to friction as claims and counter-claims are made as to whose turn it was to have a 'piece'. This is the young men's first opportunity to experience carrying St Paul. When it finishes they wring their shoulders, massaging the flesh to show the beginnings of their own *hobza*. The next step is a chance to be chosen as one of the *reffiegha* proper.

Conclusions

Carrying the statue in the *festa* fits into a developmental career, which boys aspire to from an early age. The passage from childhood to being a man in these terms, is marked by the possession of a *hobza* callus on the shoulder. With this, one's status as a *reffiegh* as achieved through developing performative competence in statue-carrying, is incorporated in the body itself. To this extent it could be regarded as a form of initiation, through which a certain category of competent men – *reffiegha* – are produced.

However, the performance differs in important ways from initiation proper. At a relatively trivial level, it is repeated annually by the same men, but more importantly it is only performed by men who are able to demonstrate their suitability through the performance of masculinity in other, everyday contexts. To this extent, the extraordinary performance of the *reffiegha* during *festa* is dependent on the everyday manifestations of being *ragel sew*. The *festa*, therefore, bridges a gap between the spectacular event and the everyday, or between performance and performativity. It also bridges a gap between the public and the personal.

The significance of the *hobza*, the *reffiegha* and the *festa* is not limited to the production of a type of masculinity. They are also important in, and because of, the public context in which they are produced. The status of the *San Pawl reffiegha* relates to their performance of an important ritual within the local and national – even international – calendar. This means that status is created with reference to people outside the confines of *Ghand Lawrenz* and the *Pawlini*, who serve as an audience for the *festa* both in the streets of Valletta, through photographs and videos and on television.

San Pawl is the commemoration of the national patron, and the moment of national conversion. It is also an expression of Catholic hegemony, and the power of the state. In carrying the statue, the *reffiegha* combines this public significance with the more intimate processes of gender identity. The *festa* combines both public performance and personal experience.

Notes

1 This chapter is based on nearly two years' fieldwork in St Paul's parish, Valletta (1992–4), during which I investigated the administration and performance of the *festa*. The research was supported by ESRC research grant number R00429134203. My thanks go to them and to Janet Carsten, Mary M. Crain, Michael Herzfeld, Felicia Hughes-Freeland, Hildi Mitchell, Miguel Vale de Almeida and three anonymous reviewers who all read and commented on earlier drafts. Thanks also to members of the Edinburgh University Social Anthropology staff seminar, who commented on a related presentation, and to the 1996 ASA Conference – particularly Rupert Cox, who stepped into the breach to read this paper when I suddenly fell ill.

2 Party politics in Malta are divided between the socialist Malta Labour Party and the Christian Democrat Nationalist Party. The Nationalists were in power 1987–96, and therefore during fieldwork.

3 Domestic violence has been seen as an index of men's real or perceived lack of power in the household.

4 The Valletta Confraternities were originally set up as guilds dedicated to the patron saint of a particular trade. Today they persist as friendly societies which ensure a decent burial for their members.

5 St Paul's Shipwreck church actually houses two relics of St Paul. The most important, and the one which is taken out during the *festa*, is the right wristbone of the apostle. This is housed in a silver arm with glass frontage to show the bone. It is believed to be miraculous and is carried on a pedestal during the procession by four minor priests.

6 Although the island of Malta is only one diocese, it has two cathedrals: the Co-Cathedral of St John's in Valletta and the Metropolitan Cathedral in Mdina.

7 This is a common feature of male sociability in Malta (see Mitchell 1996, n.d.). In many ways it can be seen as a continuation of the tradition of competitive *Ghana* folk-singing (see Sant Cassia 1991; Fsadni 1993).

Bibliography

Bell, C. (1992) *Ritual Theory: Ritual Practice*, Oxford: Oxford University Press.

Binns, C. A. P. (1979) and (1980) 'The Changing Face of Power: Revolution and Accommodation in the Development of the Soviet Ceremonial System', I and II, *Man* (ns) 14: 585–606; 15: 170–87.

Boissevain, J. (ed.) (1992) *Revitalising European Rituals*, London: Routledge.

Bourdieu, P. (1990) *The Logic of Practice*, trans. R. Nice, Cambridge: Polity Press.

Brandes, S. H. (1980) *Metaphors of Masculinity: Sex and Status in Andalusian Folklore*, Philadelphia PA: University of Pennsylvania Press.

——(1981) 'Like Wounded Stags: Male Sexual Ideology in an Andalusian Town', in S. B. Ortner and H. Whitehead (eds) *Sexual Meanings*, Cambridge: Cambridge University Press.

——(1992) 'Sex Roles and Anthropological Research in Rural Andalucia', in J. de Pina-Cabral and J. K. Campbell (eds) *Europe Observed*, London: Macmillan.

Brock-Due, V., Rudie, I. and Bleie, T. (eds) (1993) *Carved Flesh, Cast Selves: Gendered Symbols and Social Practices*, Oxford: Berg.

Butler, J. (1990) *Gender Trouble: Feminism and the Subversion of Identity*, London: Routledge.

Campbell, J. K. (1964) *Honour, Family and Patronage: A Study of Institutions and Moral Values in a Greek Mountain Community*, Oxford: Clarendon Press.

Ciarlò, J. (1995) *The Hidden Gem: St Paul's Shipwreck Collegiate Church, Valletta, Malta*, Malta: Progress Press.

Cohn, B. S. (1983) 'Representing Authority in Victorian India', in E. J. Hobsbawm and T. Ranger (eds) *The Invention of Tradition*, Cambridge: Cambridge University Press.

Connell, R. W. (1995) *Masculinities*, Cambridge: Polity Press.

Connerton, P. (1989) *How Societies Remember*, Cambridge: Cambridge University Press.

Cowan, J. K. (1991) 'Going Out for Coffee? Contesting the Grounds of Gendered Pleasures in Everyday Sociability', in P. Loizos and E. Papataxiarchis (eds) *Contested Identities: Gender and Kinship in Modern Greece*, Princeton NJ: Princeton University Press.

Crain, M. M. (1997) 'The Remaking of an Andalusian Pilgrimage Tradition: Debates Regarding Visual (Re)presentations and the Meanings of "Locality" in a Global Era', in A. Gupta and J. Ferguson (eds) *Culture, Power, Place: Explorations in a Critical Anthropology*, Durham NC: Duke University Press.

Csordas, T. J. (1990) 'Embodiment as a Paradigm for Anthropology', *Ethos*, 18, 1: 5–47.

Csordas, T. J. (ed.) (1994) *Embodiment and Experience: The Existential Grounds of Culture and Self*, Cambridge: Cambridge University Press.

Danforth, L. M. (1982) *The Death Rituals of Rural Greece*, Princeton NJ: Princeton University Press.

——(1989) *Firewalking and Religious Healing: The Anastenaria of Greece and the American Firewalking Movement*, Princeton NJ: Princeton University Press.

Davis, J. (1984) 'The Sexual Division of Religious Labour in the Mediterranean', in E. R. Wolf (ed.) *Religion, Power and Protest in Local Communities: The North Shores of the Mediterranean*, Berlin: Mouton.

de Certeau, M. (1984) *The Practice of Everyday Life*, trans. S. Rendall, Berkeley CA: University of California Press.

Dubisch, J. (1991) 'Gender, Kinship and Religion: "Reconstructing" the Anthropology of Greece', in P. Loizos and E. Papataxiarchis (eds) *Contested Identities: Gender and Kinship in Modern Greece*, Princeton NJ: Princeton University Press.

——(1995) *In a Different Place: Pilgrimage, Gender and Politics at a Greek Island Shrine*, Princeton NJ: Princeton University Press.

Foucault, M. (1977) *Discipline and Punish: The Birth of the Prison*, New York: Pantheon.

Fsadni, R. (1993) 'The Wounding Song: Honour, Politics and Rhetoric in Maltese *Ghana*', *Journal of Mediterranean Studies*, 3, 2: 335–53.

Geertz, C. (1973) 'Deep Play: Notes on the Balinese Cockfight', in C. Geertz, *The Interpretation of Cultures*, London: Hutchinson.

Gilmore, D. (ed.) (1987) *Honor and Shame and the Unity of the Mediterranean*, Washington DC: American Anthropological Association.

Goddard, V. A. (1987) 'Honour and Shame: The Control of Women's Sexuality and Group Identity in Naples', in P. Caplan (ed.) *The Cultural Construction of Sexuality*, London: Tavistock.

——(1996) *Gender, Family and Work in Naples*, Oxford: Berg.

Godelier, M. (1986) *The Making of Great Men: Male Domination and Power among the New Guinea Baruyu*, Cambridge: Cambridge University Press.

Handelman, D. (1990) *Models and Mirrors: Towards an Anthropology of Public Events*, Cambridge: Cambridge University Press.

Harris, O. (1981) 'Households as Natural Units', in K. Young, C. Wolkowitz and R. McCullagh (eds) *Of Marriage and the Market: Women's Subordination in International Perspective*, London: CSE Books.

Herdt, G. H. (ed.) (1982) *Rituals of Manhood: Male Initiation in Papua-New Guinea*, Berkeley CA: University of California Press.

Herdt, G. H. (1987) *Guardians of the Flutes: Idioms of Masculinity*, New York: Columbia University Press.

Herzfeld, M. (1984) 'The Horns of the Mediterraneanist Dilemma', *American Ethnologist*, 11: 439–54.

——(1985) *The Poetics of Manhood: Contest and Identity in a Cretan Mountain Village*, Princeton NJ: Princeton University Press.

——(1987) *Anthropology Through the Looking Glass: Critical Ethnography in the Margins of Europe*, Cambridge: Cambridge University Press.

Hirschon, R. (1981) 'Essential Objects and the Sacred: Interior and Exterior Space in an Urban Greek Locality', in S. Ardener (ed.) *Women and Space: Ground Rules and Social Maps*, London: Croom Helm.

Humphrey, C. and Laidlaw, J. (1994) *The Archetypal Actions of Ritual: A Theory of Ritual Illustrated by the Jain Rite of Worship*, Oxford: Clarendon Press.

Kapferer, B. (1988) *Legends of People, Myths of State: Violence, Intolerance and Political Culture in Sri Lanka and Australia*, Washington DC: Smithsonian Institute Press.

Kertzer, D. I. (1980) *Comrades and Christians: Religion and Political Struggle in Communist Italy*, Cambridge: Cambridge University Press.

Lane, C. (1981) *The Rites of Rulers: Ritual in Industrial Society: The Soviet Case*, Cambridge: Cambridge University Press.

Laqueur, T. W. (1990) *Making Sex: Body and Gender from the Greeks to Freud*, Cambridge MA: Harvard University Press.

Lindisfarne, N. (1994) 'Variant Masculinities, Variant Virginities: Rethinking "Honour and Shame"', in A. Cornwall and N. Lindisfarne (eds) *Dislocating Masculinity: Comparative Ethnographies*, London: Routledge.

Loizos, P. and Papataxiarchis, E. (eds) (1991) *Contested Identities: Gender and Kinship in Modern Greece*, Princeton NJ: Princeton University Press.

Lutkehaus, N. C. and Roscoe, P. B. (eds) (1995) *Gender Rituals: Female Initiation in Melanesia*, London: Routledge.

Mitchell, J. P. (1996) 'Gender, Politics and Ritual in the Construction of Social Identities: The Case of San Pawl, Valletta, Malta', unpublished PhD thesis, University of Edinburgh.

——(1997) 'A Moment with Christ: The Importance of Feelings in the Analysis of Belief', *Journal of the Royal Anthropological Institute*, 3, 1: 79–94.

——(n.d.) *Politics in Everything: Ritual, Memory and the Public Sphere in Malta*, London: Harwood.

Mizzi, S. O'R. (1981) 'Women of Senglea: The Changing Role of Urban, Working-Class Women in Malta', unpublished PhD thesis, State University of New York.

Morris, R. C. (1995) 'All Made Up: Performance Theory and the New Anthropology of Sex and Gender', *Annual Review of Anthropology*, 24: 567–92.

Moore, H. (1988) *Feminism and Anthropology*, Cambridge: Polity Press.

Mumford, L. (1970) [1938] *The Culture of Cities*, New York: Harcourt, Brace, Jovanovich.

Ortner, S. B. (1974) 'Is Female to Male as Nature is to Culture?', in M. Z. Rosaldo and L. Lamphere (eds) *Woman, Culture and Society*, Stanford CA: Stanford University Press.

Papataxiarchis, E. (1988) 'Kinship, Friendship and Gender Relations in Two East Aegean Village Communities', unpublished PhD thesis, University of London.

Parkin, D. (1992) 'Ritual as Spatial Direction and Bodily Division', in D. de Coppet (ed.) *Understanding Rituals*, London: Routledge.

Peristiany, J. G. (1965) *Honour and Shame: The Values of Mediterranean Society*, London: Weidenfeld and Nicolson.

Peteet, J. (1994) 'Male Gender and Rituals of Resistance in the Palestinian *Intifada*: A Cultural Politics of Violence', *American Ethnologist*, 21, 1: 31–49.

Pina-Cabral, J. de (1986) *Sons of Adam, Daughters of Eve: The Peasant Worldview of the Alto Minho*, Oxford: Clarendon Press.

——(1989) 'The Mediterranean as a Category of Regional Comparison: A Critical View', *Current Anthropology*, 30, 1: 399–406.

Pitt-Rivers, J. (1961) *People of the Sierra*, Chicago IL: University of Chicago Press.

——(1977) *The Fate of Shechem, or the Politics of Sex: Essays in the Anthropology of the Mediterranean*, Cambridge: Cambridge University Press.

Reiter, R. R. (1975) 'Men and Women in the South of France: Public and Private Domains', in R. R. Reiter (ed.) *Toward an Anthropology of Women*, New York: Monthly Review Press.

Rosaldo, M. Z. (1974) 'Woman, Culture and Society: A Theoretical Overview', in M. Z. Rosaldo and L. Lamphere (eds) *Woman, Culture and Society*, Stanford CA: Stanford University Press.

Said, E. (1978) *Orientalism*, Harmondsworth: Penguin.

Sant Cassia, P. (1991) '*L-Ghana*: Bejn il-Folklor u l-Habi', in T. Cortis (ed.) *L-Identita Kulturali ta'Malta*, Malta: Department of Information.

——(1993) personal communication.

Scarry, E. (1985) *The Body in Pain: The Making and Unmaking of the World*, Oxford: Oxford University Press.

Toren, C. (1990) *Making Sense of Hierarchy: Cognition and Social Process in Fiji*, London: Athlone.

Turner, V. (1969) *The Ritual Process*, Harmondsworth: Penguin.

van Gennep, A. (1960) [1909] *The Rites of Passage*, trans. M. B. Vizedom and G. L. Caffee, Chicago IL: University of Chicago Press.

Vale de Almeida, M. (1996) *The Hegemonic Male: Masculinity in a Portuguese Town*, Oxford: Berghahn Books.

Chapter 5

Nomadic performance – peculiar culture?

'Exotic' ethnic performances of WoDaaBe nomads of Niger

Mette Bovin

The 'exotic' WoDaaBe[1]

When *The WoDaaBe* (1988), a film in Granada Television's *Disappearing World* series, was shown to the public for the first time at the National Film Theatre in London, the British media wrote racy reviews about the 'exotic' WoDaaBe men, as illustrated in the following: 'an obsession with male beauty and adornment';[2] the WoDaaBe are 'obsessively vain and spend hours making themselves up to look (undeniably) beautiful';[3] 'joining the WoDaaBe at party-time when it is the menfolk who primp, preen and express their passion for personal adornment';[4] 'Don't ask "Who is a pretty boy then?" if you're among the WoDaaBe nomads of Africa: they all are and spend more time on their make-up than Michael Jackson!';[5] 'A strikingly beautiful (and suitably vain) people, they eke out an existence on the West African scrub, cleaving to strong social traditions and vivid courtship, face-painted . . . priming and pouting.'[6]

It became clear to me that in our society people are 'precoded' to only see Africa as 'exotic'. The newspapers printed nothing about the dire condition of WoDaaBe after the catastrophic Sahelian droughts of the 1970s and 1980s had killed millions of cattle and thousands of people. All the reviews focused on the beauty of these nomads. I would have liked more balanced reviews, but western media like to meet the needs of western voyeurs in search of exotic differences. As a Danish friend of mine said before I returned to the WoDaaBe in 1985: 'Oh, are you visiting the *decadent* people from the photo in *National Geographic* magazine?'[7]

So who are they, these West African nomads 'obsessed' with male beauty and vanity, striking and shocking the European eye? And what drives WoDaaBe to their extraordinary rituals?

I will answer these questions by arguing that cultural expressions such as ritual performances with deliberately cultivated elements which are recognised as appearing 'exotic' to outsiders are cultural weapons in a struggle for survival. The WoDaaBe are well aware that these exotic dances attract outsiders from Europe and America. I will show how the WoDaaBe deliberately internalise this exoticism in a strategy of what I have called 'cultural archaism' (Bovin 1985) to strengthen the boundaries of their own cultural identity in a region renowned for the complexity of its social structure and its environmental difficulties. In particular, this deliberate strategy of self-presentation is aimed at defining a social identity based on nomadism, in the face of pressures to settle and adopt the lifestyles of their neighbours. As in the case of the Balinese in Indonesia (cf. Hughes-Freeland, this volume) the media complicate this process of identity presentation, and outside interest becomes a resource for local identity politics. WoDaaBe men do not simply 'have' masculinity; they perform masculinity as a protest against state agendas, and intensify their 'exoticness' as a way of fore-grounding their difference from sedentary, agrarian Fulani who inhabit the same region.

I call the WoDaaBe 'the nomads who cultivate beauty' (Bovin 1998a), but how do they cultivate beauty, and why do they occupy themselves so much with it? Why do especially *men* (even more than women in the same society) spend enormous amounts of time, energy and money to become pretty, handsome, beautiful, 'exotic', attractive, elegant, refined and symmetrical in poor surroundings?

People of the taboos

WoDaaBe live in the 'middle of nowhere', in the West African desert, in a hot and unpleasant climate. They belong to the greater Fulani people numbering some thirty million in all.[8] The WoDaaBe, numbering around 125,000 (2–3 per cent of all Fulani), are a minority nomadic people.[9] They have a tribal system with patrilineal kinship groups, patrilineal descent and virilocality. They are divided into two big 'tribes', the Deggereeji and the Alijam, which are sub-divided into clans, sub-clans and extended families. WoDaaBe distinguish themselves strongly from semi-nomadic agro-pastoral Fulani and sedentary Fulani.[10] Pastoral nomadism is not only a form of subsistence for them – it is an entire lifestyle. The majority, about 65,000, live in Niger, but there are also substantial populations in Nigeria, Cameroun and Chad, migrating all year round with their animals.[11] Although only a small ethnic minority, the WoDaaBe travel widely over West Africa, and sometimes to Central Africa. In times of catastrophe, drought, hunger and death, many move into other countries in order to survive. It is possible to meet a few WoDaaBe in Burkina Faso, Mali, Central African Republic or in the Sudan.

WoDaaBe literally means 'The People of the Taboos'. A person is a BoDaaDo, 'a person observing *mboda* [taboo]'. The ethnic term WoDaaBe refers to their many taboos or forbidden things they observe. There are taboos in time, and taboos in space. There are taboos of names, and tabooed behaviour towards certain family members. They follow *laawol pulaaku*, 'The FulBe way' (Stenning 1959; Riesman 1977; Bovin 1998a), which stresses self-control or reserve, patience, and intelligence. WoDaaBe consider that sedentary urban Fulani have lost the most important parts of *pulaaku*, which only cattle- and sheep-herding nomads can maintain. This way is also the moral way, a spiritual as well as a physical 'path'. It is thought of as a straight line in space, with no side-paths, not bending or turning to the right or the left. The way should always be consistent and harmonious.

The cult of beauty

To WoDaaBe pastoral nomads, aesthetics is present the whole time, in everyday as well as ritual life. People talk a great deal about beauty. In fact WoDaaBe use the word every single day: '*bodum, bodum, bodum*', 'pretty, pretty, pretty' (as in the films by Bovin and Woodhead, and Herzog).[12] The WoDaaBe say of themselves that they do not want the ugly. 'We, the WoDaaBe, dislike ugly people very strongly! It is shameful to be ugly!' A WoDaaBe proverb says 'The ugly are not forgiven.' The ideal for young men and women is much the same. They should be 'red-skinned' (light-skinned), slim and narrow, with a long narrow face and limbs, 'aristocratic' aquiline nose, thin fine lips, long, thick braided hair, have wide, beautiful eyes, wear good mascara, and be clean, though neither boys nor girls should wash their whole body too often as this makes the 'power' of bodily liquids disappear. They should smell nicely of perfume or incense. A young woman should be less tall and slim than a young man – a 'round' woman is valued more highly than a skinny one.

Young men in particular invest enormous amounts of time, energy, and money in order to live up to the ideal of male beauty. And they are allowed to use time, energy and money on making themselves beautiful, as it is categorised as 'work', especially for young men. Young women spend less time, energy and money on their bodily appearance than their brothers and boyfriends do, but spend a lot of time embroidering clothes – for themselves, and for their favourite men.

There is hope even for the less beautiful. As the WoDaaBe say, 'To be _beautiful_ is good, but to have _toggu_ [charm] is _even better_!' A person who is not physically perfect can make up for it by having charm. You can increase personal charm by using magic. The use of leather-bag amulets worn around the neck, in the hair and on the skin under the clothes is common. Blue tattoos on the cheeks are known as 'charm tattoos'.

The mirror and male identity

In the bush of eastern Niger, north of Diffa town, there is less than one person per square kilometre. Most days you can walk without meeting other human beings (Bovin 1991b). Yet the first thing a young man of the WoDaaBe does in the morning is to look into his small mirror, to check and tidy up his face. He will not even go out among the cows without this morning ritual. Men put on mascara every day, in the form of kohl or antimony. They also wear jewellery and sweet perfume. They spend hours every day on their appearance, and the mirror is essential.

Apart from striving for an ideal beauty, a young WoDaaBe man should wear elegant clothes (in the right colours and latest fashion of the year), wear lots of jewellery and amulets, know the right postures of the body and move elegantly. A young WoDaaBe man has even better chances of success with women (and success in society in general) if he is a good dancer who moves correctly during all dance forms with graceful and elegant movements. If he cannot dance well, he is perhaps a good singer, which adds to the attraction of a person. A young man should also smell pleasantly of perfume or nice herbs, which he rubs on his chest, arms and neck before every performance. Charm – expressivity and charisma – is also highly valued in a young man, as are intelligence and mastery of controlled language. However, appearance and the aesthetic are central. WoDaaBe men who do not use a mirror regularly are scorned and commented on negatively. They are called lazy and not a real BoDaaDo, i.e. not a good member of the WoDaaBe.

Ethnic performance and courtship

Ethnic performance is

> a public performance involving a number of ritualized (and non-ritualized) activities – such as dancing, singing, shouting, handclapping, playing music, playing games, fighting, flirting, joking, making gestures, etc. – on a single stage at a specific time by an ethnic team of actors, in front of an audience.
>
> (Bovin 1974/5: 459)

Ethnic performances of the WoDaaBe are situations of making-up, dancing, singing, clapping, flirting and showing your best – of vanity, charm and humanness, by performers in front of an audience. This audience is often multi-ethnic in nature, and includes spectators from different ethnic groups of the region as well as Europeans and North Americans, eager to watch WoDaaBe perform. To this audience, WoDaaBe are 'exotic'. The performers know this and they play on it. They deliberately use 'strange' movements and 'cultural' outfits – but always within the 'style' of WoDaaBe material culture. Hats, feathers, clothes, shoes, jewellery and amulets should be 'WoDaaBe style' and preferably also 'à la mode' – trendy for this year's WoDaaBe style in that particular region of the Sahel.[13]

WoDaaBe themselves are often passive spectators to performances by other ethnic groups such as Kanuri, Hausa, Zerma or Tuareg, but WoDaaBe never participate in these dances or other performances. Likewise, people from other ethnic groups are not allowed to dance with WoDaaBe, and hardly ever do. Hausa-speaking peasants in Niger say of the WoDaaBe '*Babu hankali*!' ('They are not sane!'). They are believed to have a lot of *maagani* (medicine and magic) and are highly feared for their powers.

There is so much involved in a WoDaaBe dance that if we were to compare it with events in Western Europe, it would comprise dance, opera, beauty contest, lovemaking or flirting, and social gathering. Some performances are very serious, others are taken more lightly by the performers and their spectators. Sometimes dance is called *fijjo* (play), but *fijjo* has several meanings: shooting arrows from a bow when you go out in the bush hunting antelope or other game; shooting arrows at an enemy, when there is a war; playing like children do; and playing games for adults: dance, or performance in general. Dance is a serious business. Performers look forward to it and fear it at the same time. Dances are big gatherings with collective obligations. Sometimes several WoDaaBe lineages perform together, and on such occasions the famous and feared 'wife-stealing' can take place (see below).

There are several different categories of dance. They can be ranked in order of importance. The 'highest' dance is the *geerewol*, the war dance, the 'best' and 'most true' of all WoDaaBe dances and only performed by male warriors. Second in the ranking of dances is the *yaake*, the ancient magical dance. Again this is performed by men, but also involves women. It comprises a kind of 'beauty contest' in which women 'choose' the most beautiful male performer. After these two male dances come other dances like *ruume*, *borno* and *moosi*, which are performed by both men and women and play important roles in the process of social reproduction. They are opportunities to initiate courtship and marriage, as well as to celebrate births and namings. Lowest on the ranking scale come the dances which are exclusively girls' and women's dances, the *jooyde* and *jih'ere*, the 'squirrel' dance. This ranking corresponds to gender hierarchy, as women are seen as 'followers' of men.

Hirrde describes any dancing event or social gathering involving a group of young people. *Hirrde* comes from WoDaaBe 'to wake, to spend the evening, to be (in evening time)'. 'Dance' is thus always an 'evening event', even if it takes place during the daytime.

The *worso* is the greatest ritual of the year and is often a week long. It takes place when pastures are rich and abundant, so cows are well fed and people can leave home to gather in big groups of performers and spectators. It is a feast of unity, but also involves fear of separation. It combines gathering of kin with collective celebrations of naming ceremonies and marriages during the year since the last *worso*. Often between ten and thirty kin units come together for a *worso*. They camp in a special order in space for about a week, and then they each go their own way for another year. The *worso* is also an occasion for dances performed by young people of both sexes. Circles and lines of beautiful youngsters are formed. The dances take place in the bush, in a market place, or near a well, since drinking water for all the dancers is more important than a good flat stage.

Male and female dancers are expected to have an 'inner flame' and a controlled exterior during their performances. Despite experiencing deep feelings they must control their emotions in public. This discipline and self-control is required in all except the *moosi* or 'smile' dance, so called because when dancers fall into trance their faces are transformed and twisted. This trance dance differs from other dances. It is very expressive, and people 'let loose'. People from other ethnic groups watching *moosi* say 'It is not sane. Not safe', so the audience keeps its distance from the WoDaaBe dancers.

Moosi is sometimes done in connection with other dances, for instance the *ruume* dance. The *ruume* is the dance most often performed in eastern Niger. *Ruume* means 'spending the rainy season' and takes place ideally between July and September, which is the most fertile and happy of the eight seasons of the year. It is a lucky time, when the rains fall, giving food (grass) for the cattle and other animals. This eventually means that humans are well nourished and blessed with drinking milk every day. That is why many large gatherings take place directly after the rainy season between October and November, when there is a surplus. *Ruume* includes a lot of singing, both solo and in unison, and is a circular dance. The young men dance in the inner circle and the young women dance outside in a bigger circle, behind the men. Everybody faces the centre of the concentric circles. *Ruume* is always danced anti-clockwise, the dancers stepping to their right side. Men and women dance in the same direction, but at different speeds. The women often dance more slowly than the men, and as they hesitate in moving to the right, they have time to see many young men pass by them. This gives a better chance for each girl to make her choice. During the *ruume* every young girl can choose a young man by touching his back with a light movement of her hand. It is elegantly done while the women dance two-by-two in the outer circle. This movement signals: 'You are the most handsome and I'm choosing you as my lover.' Later the same evening, when the dancing has finished, the couple may disappear discreetly into the dark bush and spend the night together.

Male WoDaaBe performers are often mistaken for homosexuals by Europeans and North Americans. Some outsiders think they are transvestites. In reality this is not the case. Young WoDaaBe men perform for the sake of *the young women* of their own society, who are potential lovers or brides. They dress up and use their mirrors and fancy make-up in order to win, or steal, women from other WoDaaBe clans or lineages who are present in the same market place or at the same well at a particular time. The performances are therefore aimed at heterosexual courtship and marriage.

Dances and performances are also wife-stealing competitions, which encourages men to be attractive. Cousin – both patrilateral and cross-cousin – marriage is common. It is important to 'keep the women – and cattle – within the clan', reproduce and get children. The artistic performances are related to the 'doubleness' of the marriage system: there is *koobgal* marriage and *teegal* marriage. The first is the arranged marriage, the second is a marriage of free choice. Most WoDaaBe would like to have both a practical and a love marriage; or several of these during their lifetimes. Some people prefer the two types simultaneously, if possible, although this is easier for a man than for a woman. WoDaaBe society is one of the only societies in the world where not only men, but also women can in principle be married to two persons simultaneously. This is called *sigisbeism*, a very rare marriage form in human society. In order to win an extra wife, a man is obliged to be beautiful. He should be handsome, pretty, attractive, well-proportioned, slim, long-limbed, charming, symmetrical, perfect in body and appearance, in movements of the body, and in 'performance' – in short have *style*. He should have elegance, wakefulness, a gentleman-like quality, and be generous and unselfish.

The cult of beauty among the WoDaaBe is mainly a cult of youth. As we have seen, ugliness should be counteracted by the acquisition of charm and other virtues. Bad dancing is also socially condemned, as in the proverbs 'A clumsy dancer deserves no porridge' and 'A bad dancer is never called a brother or sister'. Nobody wishes to be close to a bad dancer. To have beauty and symmetry is necessary, but not sufficient to become a performer. Further qualifications are required. Ideally you must be a good dancer: that is an energetic and lively person. Thus a dancer should have 'scenic presence' like a good actor on a stage (Barba and Savarese 1991, Barba 1995). All young WoDaaBe men who appear in rituals are expected to be excellent dancers and clappers. They must have rhythm. During WoDaaBe dances, rhythm is majestic, and the voices are many and clear. The dancers' heads are held high, and their eyes are transformed, while they look, seek, explore, scout after beautiful young people of the opposite sex.

Body ornamentation is always symmetrical. Tattoos in particular are oriented to the vertical line in 'the middle of the face'. People say 'the middle is the best'. The ostrich feather on the hat or turban of the young male BoDaaDo is carefully placed on the axis of symmetry of his body. In the 1990s WoDaaBe men often wear one ostrich feather only, in the centre of the turban in front.[14] No matter how many ostrich feathers the youngsters wear, the feathers sway gently in the evening breezes during the dance performances. All agree proudly that the ostrich feather is a clear male, phallic symbol. No shyness or shame is expressed by young men when talking about their graceful feathers. The female pendants, the cowrie shell and the hair-pin, are two female sex symbols. Ostrich feathers and hair-pins are exhibited openly in the social gatherings. There is sometimes 'clicking' with the beads and cowrie shells hanging from the special mirrors, part of the seduction game between the sexes. The mirror, decorated with leather and beads, is used many times a day for checking one's own face and beauty. This ceremonial mirror can cost a man the price of a young cow or an ox (Bovin 1998a). Dancers also have small bottles of perfume for personal use, which can also be discretely offered as a gift to a special lover, mistress or desired person. The eye make-up made from antimony, which can shine as silver, or the pitch-black kohl, which gives a *regard de mystère*, also attracts spectators to the rituals. Black eye make-up and black lipstick stress the whiteness of the eyes and teeth, both of which are highly valued.

Flirting between women and men often takes place during dance ceremonies. Both men and women are active and take initiatives. Young women direct sharp, scrutinising glances at the young male dancers and choose from a distance who is the most handsome among the men. Young men deliver equally scrutinising glances at all the girls present. A young man who wishes to seduce and win a young woman must never be too direct. He must develop a non-aggressive, refined language. This special poetic language is called a 'sweet tongue'. This polite conversation is an art that young men learn. The seducer talks in metaphors and in poetry. If a young man is too direct or too fast, the girl may run away and listen to a more polite suitor. After a dance performance young couples may disappear into the bush in the cool of the night. The man carries a palm-leaf mat on his shoulder, and the girl walks by his side, or after him. They go into the bush to spend the night together on his mat. Young lovers (who are often also joking partners and cousins) openly show their emotions. They can hold hands no matter how many people may see them. Once married, however, there is no public show of affection. From this time on, a reserved and controlled behaviour replaces teenage manners.

'Mr WoDaaBe', not 'Miss WoDaaBe'

Beauty contests such as 'Miss Denmark' and 'Miss Universe' are often criticised for portraying women as unintelligent sex objects. But beauty contests are not degrading in WoDaaBe society. On the contrary, here in the desert it is men, not women, who are exposed in the beauty contest. To the WoDaaBe these performances are expressions of ethnic identity, and they represent pride. To the WoDaaBe, to have beauty and to expose it to the surrounding world, to exhibit the beautiful young body and soul, is a spiritual act, full of honour and dignity. It is the duty of a young man, if he is handsome, to participate in beauty competitions, and winning a competition gives great prestige. The names of male beauty contest winners are remembered for several generations by the WoDaaBe.

The WoDaaBe 'beauty contest' is *yaake* – 'the ancient dance', and the most 'magical' of all WoDaaBe dance forms (see Bovin and Woodhead 1988). The young male *yaake* stand in a long line facing the west as the evening sun goes down. They are aware of the girls who stand and watch them. The performers go up on tiptoe and move their ankles during the dance, forming a long male parade. They use special, very precise movements, especially of the feet and spinal column (Barba and Savarese 1991), and show the whiteness of their eyes and teeth through fantastic movements of the face.

Yaake involves magic, especially love-magic. *Yaake* performers dance with small movements of the body, very different from the styles performed by peasants of the same area. Whilst they move their energy down to the earth, the *yaake* dancers stretch upwards into the air, imitating long, slim, elegant birds leaving the ground. This style is not unlike European ballet dancers' depictions of 'flying' like a bird. The dancers' eyes are wide open, and roll at certain moments, and they move their throat and lips with particular vibrations, like those of a big crane or heron. The 'pre-expressivity' (Barba 1995) comes into being through the power to vibrate the throat and the lips. The magical power of large bush birds is obtained by shooting and roasting a white cattle egret (buff-backed heron), taking the blackened bones from the fire, grinding and mixing them with butter, and applying the resulting black substance to the lips. Thereby the young dancer obtains the power of expressivity. No BoDaaDo dancer believes he can perform the extremely difficult vibrations without the help of magic.

The *yaake* dance is for young men only, and it is about mastering vibrations of the throat and the lips to create a state of transformation. A really good *yaake* knows how to 'stand' on his feet in the special manner: on his toes, shifting balance as he moves from one foot to the other. He is elegantly 'flying' up into the air, as he tilts very slightly forwards while showing all his charm: the whites of his rolling eyes and flashing teeth. At the same time he turns his head from right to left, balancing the two directions in space. He remembers the three important rules for a young BoDaaDo: to unfold beauty, energy and charm – the scenic presence so valued in a dancer/performer. It requires magic as well as mere 'technique'. His ability to vibrate his lips in the right way is obtained from the power of the big long-legged bird, whose magic he must 'steal' or capture. Black lipstick for *yaake* is not just any black lipstick. Use of black powder from old radio batteries, (as in Herzog's film) for example, will not result in the same delicate vibrations of the dancer's mouth. WoDaaBe believe that those who cheat will not get the right magical result: unless the young man uses the special black 'bird lipstick' with its supernatural powers, he cannot dance the *yaake* properly.

The WoDaaBe *yaake* dancers' eyes are the most important part of the dancing body. They are used in a manner similar to that of Balinese dancers, who have a technique of widening the eyes, opening them to the maximum width and staring for some seconds before changing direction.[15] This dramatic effect is achieved by the *yaake* performing in a line in front of the young women who stand in another long line facing them. Male dancers compete for the attention of favoured girls, and their eyes, as well as focusing in space, are used expressively and to display personal charm. The formal 'jury' of three girls considers the eyes first and foremost when choosing the winner of the annual *yaake* dance. The blinking of the eyes, and the showing of the whiteness of the eyes and teeth, are the most important things to be mastered by a male dancer. The movements of the entire body, its grace and elegance, and its capacity to go up on tiptoe in the right way, are of course also important. The judges also attend carefully to the shape of the body, which ideally should be long and slim, but not skinny.

Dance is like war

WoDaaBe say 'Dance is like war!' (*'Fijjo kamma habre!'*). It is a serious matter. Male dancers are not just 'showing their beauty in a long line', as articles in popular western women's magazines state (*Elle* 1989). Performers often push their neighbouring dancers backwards in order to be seen better by spectators, as they move forward on elegant tiptoes. 'It is a war-like situation', participants have told me afterwards, 'Very tiring indeed!' One woman referred to making-up and dance as 'work' for the men of the clan.[16]

Yaake dancers all try to be best at impressing the young women. The women stand in a crowd at a distance. They look shy, but they are in fact active and important spectators. The special jury, or *suhboyki* (the choosers) is a ritual office with fixed sets of behaviour, and is always composed of three especially beautiful and important young women who will choose not 'Miss' but 'Mr WoDaaBe' of the year. The jury always performs its ritual in the same manner. The three girls walk in a line, one after the other, with the girl of highest status – the daughter of a male champion, for example – in front. Girls from one clan walk slowly up to the dancers of the opposite clan and choose the winner. Then it is the turn of the opposite clan. Another three *suhboyki* girls walk ritually across the same arena and make their choice among the male dancers of their 'enemy' clan (competitors). As they walk they look down at the sand, but not before taking a sharp look from a distance before moving close to the line of men. They walk along the ranks of male dancers, the first girl swinging her right arm. The whole audience shouts with joy (as at a football match) as she stops in front of the most handsome man. He is the winner and gets a prestigious title.

He does not, however, sleep with the girls from the jury during the night, as is claimed in the *Elle* article. Other women's magazines tell of love-orgies, of a real-life 'Sodom and Gomorrah', while journalists paint a paradise-like image of WoDaaBe nomads. These popular articles are superficial, and often factually incorrect. The beauty parades during *yaake* dances do not usually end in sex, though some of the dancers may find partners.[17]

During other dances, performers are forbidden to have sex, which does not fit with the strict rules of self-discipline and of energy which must be used instead for making oneself pretty and charming. These are the more serious dances, which take from three days to a week to perform. The most famous of them is the *jeerewol* or *geerewol*: the war dance. The dance takes the form of a competition between two opposing clans. In the Diffa region these are the Suudu-Suka'el and Jiijiiru clans. Because of droughts and political conflicts in the area, the *jeerewol* was not performed from 1969 to 1993, but in the autumn of 1994 it was taken up again. The two clans alternately 'host' the dance, and the men from each clan take turns in 'stealing' women from the opposite clan. As WoDaaBe often say, 'the women always follow after the men'.[18] In eastern Niger, Suudu-Suka'el men steal women from the Jiijiiru, and vice-versa. In western Niger Yamanko'en men steal wives from the Kassawsaawa clan, and vice-versa. The male dancers, who must be handsome 'warriors' (although they do not go to actual war), appear with red-painted bodies, or red faces, necks and torsos, for the dance. Red is the colour of war and death. Dancers wear white beads over their red torsos. Each dancer wears a white ostrich feather in the turban, and carries a ceremonial 'axe' in the right hand. This is a light axe with a rectangular head and wooden handle, but not one which could be used in real war, since it is too light and not at all sharp.

Performance and identity

Ethnic identity is formed, reproduced and strengthened during dance performances in Niger. Dancing is not 'just for fun', as is often the case in western dancing. As Hughes-Freeland, writing on Javanese performances, expresses it,

> dancing is more than physical activity. . . . As in many societies, dancing is a serious activity. . . . Dancing is a visual metaphor for effective access to, and understanding of, the exemplary forms of being Javanese.
>
> (1997: 56)

This is also true for the WoDaaBe. WoDaaBeness is seriously attained through dancing. Sometimes WoDaaBe have come up to me after a dance and said 'Now you are becoming *debbo* BoDaaDo [WoDaaBe woman]!' It is at the heart of WoDaaBe identity to dance with other WoDaaBe.

The semi-nomadic agro-pastoral FulBe (of Niger, Nigeria, Chad and Cameroun) practise a ceremony called *sorro*. It is often held in market places, and is a test of male endurance, patience, bravery and indifference to pain. It includes a beating with a huge stick which is so severe that the young male dancers sometimes die (Bovin 1974/5, 1991a). The *sorro* is a true rite of passage, an initiation ceremony that 'produces' men.

The *sorro* performances are tests of enduring and surviving pain, and differ considerably from those of the nomadic WoDaaBe, which are concerned with beauty and appearance. The WoDaaBe dances and other performances are not violent but 'soft', although they also involve heavy competition. They are also obligatory.

Do FulBe and WoDaaBe performances have anything in common? The performances of both ethnic groups are related to courtship, betrothal, mating, marriage and wife-stealing. As such they are 'marriage partner dances' which offer 'access' to the opposite sex. They are also ethnic performances. Both groups speak the same language, Fulfulde, and know and observe the same rules of *pulaaku*, the moral code. Nomadic WoDaaBe and semi-nomadic FulBe share cultural key concepts, like *laawol pulaaku*, the Fulani way. Yet the dances demonstrate the differences between the two. For WoDaaBe, this involves elaborate demonstrations of beauty.

The WoDaaBe often say '*We* are the most beautiful people in the world!' Their dancing asserts this aesthetic supremacy in which WoDaaBe place themselves at the top of an ethnic prestige scale (Bovin 1985). This beauty is embodied, not just in the special performances, but also through everyday bodily comportment. It is a question of posture as much as adornment. WoDaaBe walk and ride on their animals in an upright position. This gives straightness of the body, the importance of a 'vertical' posture being emphasised in the *yaake* dance. This posture contrasts with farmers of the same region, who work with a bent back, using the hoe in the field which produces a V-shaped position of the body, making it less aesthetically pleasing to WoDaaBe eyes.

WoDaaBe often make linguistic comparisons between themselves and wild birds. Male dancers seek to obtain the qualities of the ostrich, eagle, heron and crane. Sometimes they say 'We build a nest in the bush and then we fly off again'. Yet in the act of cultivating beauty, nature is appropriated. It operates as a 'stamp' of culture on the body, embellished with tattoos, paints, embroidered clothes and jewellery.

Media and change in performance

WoDaaBe culture is not 'traditional' in the sense of being a static culture, as some observers believe. On the contrary, WoDaaBe fashion often changes in its shapes, forms, colours and materials. WoDaaBe wear jewellery made of leather, brass, copper and aluminium, although I have never seen gold employed.[19] A leather loincloth is used by young men on all important ceremonial occasions where cotton trousers are banned. In the old days the man's tunic was made from indigo cloth, hand-woven and hand-dyed. In 1968, when I first met WoDaaBe in eastern Niger, all the WoDaaBe used dark blue, indigo-dyed clothes. Now, thirty years later, only very few WoDaaBe use indigo cloth, and for feasts only. Almost everyone uses black factory-woven and dyed cotton cloth imported from China, since it is cheaper than indigo cloth. Women wear dark skirts and blouses. In 1968 young women's blouses were very short, like 'bolero' blouses, but in the 1980s and 1990s their blouses have become much longer, reaching to the waist or hips, and the belly is no longer shown publicly.

Performances also change. In Dakoro and Niamey (the capital city) the *geerewol* has been undergoing a kind of 'inflation' since Niger's television sometimes comes along to film the WoDaaBe dance as a 'folkoristic event'. Often WoDaaBe from Dakoro perform at agricultural shows, opening ceremonies, etc. Film teams have added a new and often distorted picture of WoDaaBe dances (cf. Crain, this volume).[20]

The appearance of modern cinema has also brought other changes to WoDaaBe performances and clothes. To be light-skinned is to be beautiful and superior in WoDaaBe eyes. To be beautiful is to the WoDaaBe to be 'red-skinned', but although WoDaaBe regard themselves as 'the most beautiful people in the world', some WoDaaBe have told me that the 'Hindus' are more beautiful than themselves, referring to people from the Indian subcontinent. In West Africa 'Hindu' (i.e. Hindi) films are popular in big cities and are even shown in smaller towns, with Indian ladies dancing in beautiful gardens, with rocks, rubies and love-stories. Film stars with 'red' skin and plenty of jewellery and nice clothes are highly admired, as are men with 'beautiful turbans, and nice handsome faces and fine noses'. Some WoDaaBe began to imitate Hindu headdresses in the 1970s and 1980s.

Self-exhibition and cultural archaism

One may wonder why the WoDaaBe continue to reproduce the 'exotic'; why they deliberately show their art in farming villages and market places, the most public of all spaces in West Africa. Why do they not stick to performing 'at home' in the bush, in their own nomadic family camps, exclusively for other WoDaaBe?

This self-exhibition of 'strange culture' is highly political, and can be used as a strategic weapon. WoDaaBe extravagance is part of their cultural resistance. Dances, songs and beauty parades are 'cultural weapons' against their increasing marginalisation.

The WoDaaBe are being squeezed from the north (by desertification), from the south (by agricultural colonisation of the Sahel), from the east (by Tubu nomads) and from the west (by Tuareg nomads). They are being chased out into drier and drier desert habitats. They are losing capital, i.e. their animals. Zebu cattle, sheep, goats and camels die in years of drought. There are also strong pressures on nomads to 'settle down and become civilised like us, the Hausa and Kanuri and Zerma in the Republic of Niger and Nigeria and Chad' (Bovin 1985, 1997). Settled farmers tend to win when there are conflicts over grazing or agricultural land. The WoDaaBe fear the way of life of settled FulBe, who 'have lost the Way' (*laawol pulaaku*), the moral code which to them is linked with true cattle nomadism. It is necessary for the WoDaaBe to 'show their existence' more clearly now, more visibly.

This is why the WoDaaBe continue to reproduce 'the exotic' and why they deliberately perform in farming villages and market places as well as at their distant bush camps. Being deliberately exotic is one of their strategies.

WoDaaBe dances are ethnic performances par excellence. The young men's leather trousers or loincloths are not only sexy but political, proclaiming the message: 'We are different. We are old-fashioned. We are of the bush. We are not like settled Muslims. We are WoDaaBe!' In order to remain a nomadic pastoralist, you must constantly 'fight' against various sedentarisation pressures. You are up against the governments of four nation states as well as against settled farmers in these same countries. Performers are transmitting ethnic as well as religious messages to the surrounding peoples. The ethnic performance can be seen as a political weapon besides having an aesthetic value for WoDaaBe performers and spectators. These visually extravagant performances of dance, music and song form part of the survival strategy of an ethnic minority that is continually being chased out into more and more arid parts of the desert, continually being marginalised.

This is why WoDaaBe cultural performances not only endure, but have become more and more colourful and extravagant since the 1970s. They must almost 'overdo' their ethnic manifestations *vis-à-vis* the outside world in order to remain WoDaaBe, to be allowed to continue as nomads migrating in the bush. So we see picturesque dances, songs and feasts in the middle of Diffa town and Zinder town. We watch WoDaaBe 'dances' in front of Nigerian television teams in Dakoro. WoDaaBe troups have even performed in Europe: in Paris for the last three decades, and in the 1990s in Denmark, Sweden, Belgium and Holland. Since 1990 there has been strong competition among WoDaaBe migrant labourers living in and near the capital city Niamey to join WoDaaBe tours to Europe.

Conclusions

In western societies we are precoded to read Africa as exotic. Nomadic WoDaaBe rituals fit well into our stereotype of exotic otherness. Men's dances, painted masks and strange eye movements are famous outside WoDaaBeland, and have been portrayed in western magazines from the *National Geographic* to *Elle*, in documentary films by directors such as Robert Gardner and Werner Herzog, and also in film dramas.[21] Niger Television regularly broadcasts WoDaaBe performances under labels like 'Bororo geerewol' and 'Dances des Peuls Bororo'.

I have tried to demystify the exoticness of these dances, to demonstrate their significance in the production of male identity, and in the processes of courtship, marriage and procreation. I have also argued that the dances demarcate the ethnic space of WoDaaBeness, in relation both to neighbouring peoples and the state. I see these cultural expressions as true cultural weapons. They are strategies of survival for nomadic peoples across the globe. WoDaaBe 'cultural archaism' (Bovin 1985) is thus a deliberate 'weapon' which is linked to their reproduction of WoDaaBe identity management, which in turn is linked to their fight for economic, political and land rights and the continuation of *ngaynaaka*, the pastoral nomadic life in the 'sweet bush' (*ladde beldum*). WoDaaBe culture is constantly changing, with inventions of new 'archaic' elements, or 'active archaisation', according to fashion in the bush. However, there remains a continuity and essential kernel which is not touched or moved: the moral ideas of the WoDaaBe way: *laawol pulaaku*.

Notes

1 My thanks to Felicia Hughes-Freeland and Mary M. Crain for their valuable comments on a previous draft of this chapter, and to Felicia Hughes-Freeland and Jon Mitchell for helping to redraft the English in parts.

2 *Guardian*, 27 July 1988.

3 *Sunday Times*, 24 July 1988.

4 Linda Grant, 'Making WoDaaBe Whoopee', *Evening Standard*, 22 July 1988.

5 Tom Ferguson, *Sunday Telegraph*, 24 July 1988.

6 *Independent*, 27 July 1988.

7 *National Geographic*, (USA) 164, 4, October 1983.

8 The Fulani live in eighteen African countries: Nigeria, Niger, Chad, Cameroun, Central African Republic, Sudan, Senegal, Sierra Leone, Gambia, Mali, Mauritania, Guinea Conakry, Guinea Bissau, Burkina Faso, Ghana, Togo, Benin and Ivory Coast. They are called 'FulBe' in their own language, 'Peuls' in Francophone countries, 'Pulaar' in Senegal, Gambia and Mauritania, 'Fula' in Guinea, and 'Fellata' in the Sudan. For a pioneering analysis of ethnic identity, see Barth 1969.

9 Thanks to my French colleague Patrick Paris, in Zinder, Niger, for this statistical information.

10 WoDaaBe are 'opportunistic' rather than 'conservative' (Sandford 1983) in their pastoral strategy. WoDaaBe also have no fixed houses, and exhibit the most 'traditional culture' of all Fulani.

11 Bovin 1974/5, 1979, 1985, 1990a, 1990b, 1991a, 1991b, 1995, 1998a.
12 A person can be *bodum*, and an object can be *bodum* ('beautiful' in the Fulfulde language). The WoDaaBe noun for beauty is *wodde*. 'To be' (*na wodi*) and 'to be beautiful (*na wodi*) is expressed by the same term. The negation *wo'da*, means 'ugly', or 'that which should disappear'. Ugliness is almost like non-existence.
13 Differences in fashion over time and space are described in Bovin 1998a.
14 In 1968 I saw young men wearing lots of ostrich feathers placed in a harmonious circle all around the conical straw hat.
15 'Both in Bali . . . and in the Peking Opera . . . the eyes are directed . . . higher than they normally are in daily life' (Barba and Savarese 1991: 106).
16 This occurs in my film about WoDaaBe perfomances, which is not yet edited.
17 Werner Herzog's (1991) film shows a young couple talking about sex, giving the viewer a distorted impression of verbal liberty.
18 Specific women's dances are called by animal names, but specific men's dances are not called by animal names (Bovin 1998b).
19 This precious metal they leave to the settled Muslim farmers of the Sahel: Kanuri, Shuwa Arabs and Hausa, who are very fond of gold, and buy it in Mecca.
20 When WoDaaBe women make '*yaake*' eyes in front of a television camera in the 1990 film as a provocation, this turns WoDaaBe performance into something non-WoDaaBe, as *yaake* eyes are normally only made by men.
21 Such as *Lelee*, a film drama by Ahmadou Kanta about a WoDaaBe girl who is the first-born 'taboo child'.

Bibliography

Barba, E. and Savarese, N. (1991) *A Dictionary of Theatre Anthropology: The Secret Art of the Performer*, a Centre for Performance Research Book, London and New York: Routledge.

Barba, E. (1995) *The Paper Canoe: Introduction to Theatre Anthropology*, London: Routledge.

Barth, F. (ed.) (1969) *Ethnic Groups and Boundaries: The Social Organisation of Culture Difference*, Bergen: Universitetsforlag; London: Allen and Unwin.

Beckwith, C. and van Offelen, M. (1984) *Nomads of Niger*, London: Collins.

Bovin, M. (1974/5) 'Ethnic Performances in Rural Niger: An Aspect of Ethnic Boundary Maintenance', *Folk*, Journal of the Danish Ethnographic Society, vol. 1617, 459–74.

——(1979) 'Etniske Symboler i et Afrikansk Kongedøme: Borno' (ed. Flemming Højlund, in Danish with an English summary) *Hikuin*, vol. 5, Moesgård Museum, Aarhus University, Denmark.

——(1985) 'Nomades "Sauvages" et Paysans "Civilisés": WoDaaBe et Kanuri au Borno', *Journal des Africanistes*, 55, 12, 53–73; Paris: Musée de l'Homme.

——(1990a) 'Relations Interethniques au Borno (Nigeria et Niger): Culture Matérielle et Dichotomie Homme/Femme', *Relations Interethniques et Culture Matérielle dans le Bassin du Lac Tchad* (Actes du IIIème Colloque Méga-Tchad) 103–20; Paris: Orstom.

——(1990b) 'Nomads of the Drought: Fulbe and WoDaaBe Nomads between Power and Marginalisation in the Sahel of Burkina Faso and Niger Republic', in M. Bovin and L. Manger (eds) *Adaptive Strategies in African Arid Lands*, Uppsala: Scandinavian Institute of African Studies, 29–57.

——(1991a) ' "Mariages de la Maison" et "Mariages de la Brousse" dans les Sociétés Peule, WoDaaBe et Kanuri autour du Lac Tchad', in N. Echard (ed.) *Les Relations Hommes-femmes dans le Bassin du Lac Tchad* (Actes du IVe Colloque Méga-Tchad) Paris: CNRS/Orstom.

——(1991b) 'Spor i Sandet og Graesset: Om Begrebet "Bush" hos Fulani Nomaderne', in S. Dybbroe, P. B. Möller, A. Oleseon, E. Vestergaard and T. A. Vestergaard (eds) *Klaus Khan Baba: En Etnografisk Kalejdoskopi Tilegnet Klaus Ferdinand den 19 April 1991*, Aarhus: Aarhus Universitets-forlag, 134–53.

——(1995) 'Pastoralists, Droughts, and Survival in West Africa', in T. Negash and L. Rudebeck (eds) *Dimensions of Development with Emphasis on Africa*, Uppsala: The Nordic Africa Institute and Forum for Development Studies, Uppsala University.

——(1997) 'Marginalised Nomads of the Sahel: The WoDaaBe', in *The Indigenous World 1996–7*, Copenhagen, IWGIA, 252–6.

——(1998a) *Nomads who Cultivate Beauty: WoDaaBe Dances and Visual Arts in Niger*, Uppsala: The Nordic Africa Institute.

——(1998b) 'La Belle Vache: Chansons d'Hommage aux Animaux et aux Etres Humains chez les WoDaaBe du Niger', in *L'Homme et l'Animal dans le Bassin du Lac Tchad*, Séminaire du Réseau Méga-Tchad, Orléans, 15–17 October 1997. Paris: Editions de l'Orstom.

Dupire, M. (1962) *Peuls Nomades: Etude Descriptive des WoDaaBe du Sahel Nigérien*, Paris: Musée de l'Homme.

Fisher, A. (1987) *Africa Adorned*, London: Collins Harvill.

Hughes-Freeland, F. (1997) 'Consciousness in Performance: A Javanese Theory', *Social Anthropology*, 5, 1, 55–68.

Riesman, P. (1977) *Freedom in Fulani Social Life: An Introspective Ethnography* (translated from the French by Martha Fuller), Chicago IL and London: University of Chicago Press.

Sandford, S. (1983) *Management of Pastoral Development in the Third World*, New York: Wiley.

Stenning, D. (1959) *Savannah Nomads: A Study of the WoDaaBe Pastoral Fulani of Western Bornu Province, Northern Region, Nigeria*, London: Oxford University Press.

Newspapers and magazines

Elle (France) no. 2286, 30 October 1989, 20–34, 'La Parade d'Amour des Bororos du Niger: Les Plus Beaux pour aller Dancer', by Philippe Trétiack.

Evening Standard, 22 July 1988, 'Making WoDaaBe Whoopee', by Linda Grant.

Independent, 27 July 1988, 'Unsettling the Nomads', by W. Stephen Gilbert.

National Geographic (USA) 164, 4, October 1983, 482–509, 'Niger's WoDaaBe: People of the Taboo', by Carol Beckwith.

Films

Nomades du Soleil (1953–4) black and white. Henry Brandt, director and caméra. Musée d'Ethnographie de Neuchtel, Switzerland.

Deep Hearts (1979) 53 mins, colour. Robert Gardner, director. Film Study Centre, Harvard University.

WoDaaBe – les Bergers du Soleil ['Herdsmen of the Sand'] (1988/91) 52 mins, colour. Werner Herzog, director. Arion Production, Paris and Werner Herzog Productions, Munich and Antenne 2, Canal Plus, France.

Lelee (1990) Ahmadou Kanta, writer and director, and Annique Legall, director. Paris.

The WoDaaBe (1988) 16mm, 53 mins. Film 44, *Disappearing World*, Granada Television. Leslie Woodhead, producer, and Mette Bovin, anthropologist.

På Tchad-söens Bund. En Film om et Venskab (1992) video, 35 mins. Statens Filmcentral, Copenhagen. Written and directed by Mette Bovin.

Ethnic Co-existence in Nigeria (1995) video, 29 mins. Produced, filmed and directed by Mette Bovin. Nordiska Afrikainstitutet, Uppsala.

Chapter 6

Making persons in a global ritual?

Embodied experience and free-floating symbols in Olympic sport

Ingrid Rudie

Introduction

The particular analytical concern of this chapter is to identify the element of ritualisation in Olympic sport.[1] In order to achieve this, I shall start from how the bodily nature of sport makes it both easily communicable and highly esoteric. Core questions will be how far symbols of the person as communicated in the arena and in the media can be shared and extended, and indeed, whether there is such a thing as a global ritual. These questions are of course related to the broader understanding of symbols and ritual as vehicles of shared understanding, and to the highly contextual character of meaning-making.[2] The questions further invite a careful sorting out of the discourses as well as the pre-discursive fields of experience in which various sports are embedded.

The issue of gender is of central concern in my analysis, because I argue that sport exhibits in a distilled manner a split message about gender equality and inequality. In everyday experience this split tends to be blurred by the complexity of practices and discourses in modern society. In sport it stands out clearly because an ongoing struggle for gender equality coexists with a strict set of rules designed to keep biologically defined male and female categories apart and pure.[3]

My focus is on various negotiations – in a wide sense of the term – about the gender issue in different disciplines, and the symbolic repercussions of particular athletes and particular events.

The Olympics: global event and multi-layered performance

A central ideological theme of the Olympic Games, dating right back to the days of de Coubertin,[4] is barrier-breaking, in the sense of both stretching human achievement, and of furthering global under-standing. 'Globalisation' and 'performance' are two general concepts that seem promising in order to approach an analysis of the meanings and actions of the games. Friedman has argued that 'fragmentation' and 'modernist homogenisation' are two constitutive trends of global processes.[5] The Olympic arrangement is a global and globalising event in this sense: it represents fragmentation and homogenisation at the institutional or social structural level as well as on the level of meaning. It brings together different experiential worlds, splits open the local world of the host society, and grounds the individual in circuits of communication and recognition on both local and global scale. Globalisation, then, is essentially about the membership of the person in the world, and therefore about identity. It is also about conceptions of how particular places can become sites of events of extraordinary importance. In 1994 and the years before there was a great deal of excitement over the fact that the small provincial town of Lillehammer was to become the focus of global attention.

MacAloon, who pioneered the anthropological analysis of the Olympics, has described the Games as a multi-layered public event in which genres of performance lie embedded within one another in Chinese box fashion (MacAloon 1984: 253ff.). In his scheme 'spectacle' is the most inclusive genre, containing within its boundary other genres like 'festival', 'ritual' and 'game'. According to MacAloon, spectacles are grandiloquent occasions linking performer and audience, and involving excitement, but not 'faith' as a ritual is expected to convey: 'Ritual is a duty, spectacle a choice' (1984: 243). This implies that in a spectacle performers and audience are free to 'read' messages at will, combine images and construct their meanings.

Sport as a link between the local and the global

The Olympic Games consists of a host of activities and a heteroge-neous range of interests besides sport,[6] but sport is the core activity and basic legitimation. The issues of sport and global membership converge on the person in a particular manner. Elite athletes fulfil the barrier-breaking ideal of the Games in both senses of the word – of stretching achievement, and of crossing international boundaries. In the not-too-distant past, before the age of easy travel, television and cyberspace, the champion brought a sensation of global membership to his (it was normally his, not her, in those days) home district, the glory from the arena 'out there' rubbed off on the athlete's – often – provincial birthplace.[7] In a certain sense we can look upon elite athletes as symbolic spearheads to global membership before the concept of globalisation was invented. This brings into focus the particular symbolic convenience of sport. On one level, sport has an unequalled power to fascinate across social and cultural boundaries. On another level, different disciplines of sport carry specific meanings that are not easily communicated in any full extent outside the ranks of practitioners and fans. Both these features can be traced back to the same roots – to fundamental properties of sportive activities. These are bodily activities following universally shared principles of human kinetics. These kinetic experiences are in part pre-discursive or unarticulated, at the same time as their universality makes them easily understood and communicated on a certain level. But specific disciplines have also developed in close conjunction with specific local cultural traditions, and carry a load of tacit social memory in their capacity of 'incorporating practices'. in Connerton's sense.[8] On this level the experiences of movement, place and relationships merge in a specific blend that becomes partly inaccessible to outsiders. On this level, then, meanings separate.

The reader may now justifiably ask whether there is any important distinction to be drawn between elite sport in general and Olympic sport in particular. The Olympic Games are unique among sports events in the degree to which they bring together different disciplines – we thus have the unique possibility of studying both convergence and divergence of meaning. In one respect, meaning is negotiable and changeable. But it may not be easily *ex*changeable. Symbols may be widely shared and may expand their impact, but their content may still to a large extent be untranslatable because they are rooted in experience that is at the same time local, specific and partly wordless. The symbolic entity in focus in the following analysis will be the images of female athletes, and how they may possibly nourish ritual identification as well as (re-)construction of meaning both within and across experiential fields.

Some challenges to the study of ritual

There has been a profound disagreement in the literature between different ways of stressing what ritual is 'about'. One issue, stemming from the Durkheimian paradigm, sees ritual as acts of worship (of the 'sacred' or of 'society'). Another issue has been about ritual as either an act in itself, or an aspect of acts. The processual form 'ritualisation' has recently been proposed by Catherine Bell (1992) in her book on ritual theory and ritual practice, and this has been seized upon by Humphrey and Laidlaw in an effort to free the study of ritual from what they see as fruitless dichotomies (1994: 64).

Two main points in Bell's book are of particular interest. First, she stresses ritual's interwovenness with other social action. Rather than seeing ritual as a distinct class of action, she suggests moving the stress from ritual to ritualisation in order to accomplish the understanding of this interwovenness. The second important point is the way in which ritualisation is tied to the person, as

> a purposeful or 'strategic' . . . production of ritualised agents, persons who have an instinctive knowledge of [these schemes] embedded in their bodies, in their sense of reality, and in their understanding of how to act in ways that both maintain and qualify the complex micro relations of power.
>
> (Bell 1992: 221)

Another pertinent formulation stresses the sense of fit between the main spheres of experience: body, community and cosmos (Bell 1992: 109).

Although the stress on strategy and the link to power structures raised by Bell can certainly be questioned, and the outcome of such questioning will among other things depend on the understanding of 'strategy' and 'power', in this chapter I concentrate on the way in which ritualisation can be seen to instil dispositions in the person. This echoes a host of established and emergent theorising on the embodiment of culture as it can be approached from different angles.[9]

A need for distinctions?

In recent literature there have been several attempts to explore the fruitfulness of distinctions between performative genres, and between ritual and other more truly performative genres (Bell 1992; Humphrey and Laidlaw 1994; Hughes-Freeland 1998).

Sport is performance, in any normal sense of the term, and it also lends itself to more specific epithets like 'drama' and 'ritual'. Gusfield has likened the sports contest to a drama, in an attempt to explain its powers of fascination. The performances dramatise victory and loss that do not always seem 'just' from the point of view of the athletes' skill and effort; a whole lifetime's drama about choices, loss and victory can be exemplified in one single competition; and sports contests may remind the spectators of mythical themes such as the Biblical narrative of David and Goliath. Last but not least, the drama consists mainly of physical activities that belong in a universally shared repertoire of experience (Gusfield 1987).[10] The dramatic and textual character of the contest make it speak immediately to the spectators' own understanding of 'reality'. In fact, Gusfield draws on two levels in his effort to explain the fascination of sport: on the most universal kinetic experiences, and on the experience of loss and reward which may be less universal, probably more in tune with a western idea of what connection there ought to be between effort and reward. His notion of drama connotes to the two senses of drama that Turner has distinguished: social drama as 'an objectively isolable sequence of social interaction of a conflictive, competitive or agonistic type' (1986: 33) and 'dramas at their simplest' as 'literary compositions that tell a story usually of human conflict, by means of dialogue and action, and are performed by actors' (1986: 27).

Rostas (1998) underlines the difficulty of distinguishing empirically between ritualisation and performativity, but still maintains that they should be seen as analytically distinguishable processes, ritual as a way of acting that is habitual or has become part of habitus (1998: 89), a stance in which actors renounce being 'the authors of their actions' (1998: 90). In contrast, performativity is seen as [often having] the sense of 'loading an act with meaning, even if overdoing it, of above all insisting on 'meaning to mean' (1998: 90).

Gusfield's conception of drama which spans the range between embodied experience and narrative, Rostas' model of acts that oscillate between ritualisation and performativity, and my discussion above on implications of the bodily nature of sport have something in common in that they echo a two-level attack on the issue of experience and the production of meaning. This is where we have to start an attempt at sorting out some strands of ritual and performative genres in the Olympics. Yet another support can be found in Csordas' observation that the emergent anthropological literature on 'the body' would do well to distinguish more clearly between the body as either 'empirical thing' or 'analytic theme' on the one hand, and 'embodiment' as the existential ground of culture and self on the other (1994: 6). Using Csordas' distinction, we may say that the body as empirical theme lends itself to textualisation and symbol analysis, while the concept of embodiment opens the access to an analysis of preconceptual experience. Embodied experience is linked to convictions of 'truth' and 'nature', but is not easily given to interpretation. In the same manner, ritual is concerned with belief and participation rather than with 'meaning'. Therefore, meaning is open to negotiation and (creative) interpretation, while experience-based understanding is to some extent incommunicable.

The stress on embodiment will bring out the pole of ritualisation, in which experience and commitment take precedence over meaning and communication. The stress on the body (and its performances) as an empirical theme will bring out the pole of drama, symbolisation and the negotiation of meaning.

We can now revert to the question posed above: whether there is such a thing as a global ritual. The most obvious example in the Olympic Games would be the grand ceremonies on the opening and closing days, as well as the medal ceremonies at the end of each day. These are rituals in the classical sense, and have also been analysed as such (MacAloon 1984; Puijk, in press). My concern here will be more with discovering the oscillation between ritualisation and performativity in specific competitions, adopting what may be called a more 'embryonic' view of ritual. To attempt a preliminary statement starting from this approach, I suggest that the Olympics can be seen as a conglomeration of ritualised sequences that mirror complexity and even contradictions between various discourses and experiential worlds. This certainly applies when we see the Olympic arrangement in its full scope, as a mega event[11] including a host of activities besides athletics.

A model of ritualisation of the Olympics

If we narrow the scope down to athletics as core activity, ritualisation can be identified in different facets. Any specific competition can be viewed as a complex sequence with core activities directly involving performers and spectators in devoted participation, and symbolic spin-offs that float more freely across experiential fields. As a preliminary tenet, we can identify ritualisation as that which nourishes faith and deep involvement, and dramatisation as that which nourishes spectatorship and symbolic spin-off. These further suggest two levels in the cultural reproduction of persons: the level of 'cultural nature' or *habitus* (Bourdieu 1977; Bell 1992; Hughes-Freeland 1998) and the level of social image. It can further be argued that both levels (if levels they be) in their turn nourish the particular – and sometimes conflicting – discourses concerning truth and justice in society at large.

Women's entrance into elite sport in general, and into Olympic sport in particular, has shifted from the role of mere spectators to that of also being participants. Gradually, they have been admitted to one sport after another. The main argument in their thrust for participation has been about fairness and equality; the struggle for participation in sport has been one version of the general struggle for gender equalisation in society at large.

However, the principle of equality acquires ambiguity in sport, as men's and women's competitive ranks must necessarily remain separate. The biological properties of men and women become the final sorting principle. The importance of this principle lies behind the introduction in 1968 of sex testing in elite sport. Sex and gender, 'biology' and 'culture', are conflated in an emic concept of 'nature'. The resistance to women's participation in competitive sport was explicitly grounded in arguments about nature, be it conventional moral and aesthetic views on the proper 'female nature', or medical beliefs about the frailty of the female physique. The symbolic importance of keeping genders separate is clearly demonstrated in the aesthetic style of figure skating, one of the examples that I will analyse below. According to Abigael Feder, this discipline calls on athletic qualities that are at least as well developed in women as in men, like flexibility and acrobatic skill. In other words, men have hardly any biological advantages above women, which has made it necessary to put such great stress on conventional femininity in order to ensure the difference between the sexes (Feder 1995: 23).

Sacred principles of competition – the ritual agenda

Every competition has its ritual agenda regulated by unbreakable rules designed in order to guarantee absolute fairness. These principles concern the purity of categories – of the person, and of interactional modes. In his book *Mortal Engines*, Hoberman suggests that the great concern about doping in sport can be understood as an obsession with purity and the genuine that comes as a reaction to civilisation: there is a need to see athletes as 'the last true performers' (Hoberman 1992:

111). The same argument can be made about gender in sport. Discourses about nature also relate to equality as regards fairness. The natural athletic body must not be enhanced by steroids, and the pure *female* athlete, in addition, must not be contaminated by a too-high proportion of male hormones. But the careful biological sorting between male and female, undertaken in the name of fairness, reminds participant and public of a 'truth' that may nourish the conflated concept of nature, and threaten the process of gender equalisation elsewhere in society.[12]

The athlete's body stands in the midst of the triad of body, cosmos and community as it has been formulated by Bell (1992: 109). The athletes themselves are expected to adhere to the principles of sociality and personal purity, and the spectators are their co-believers and judges. These rules approximate a cosmic order; they are not contested, although they are sometimes broken in highly subversive acts like drug taking or other attempts at cheating. When discovered, these acts lead to counter-acts as offenders are excluded from future competitions and victories won under false pretences are annulled. The counter-acts are true acts of ritual purification.

In order to further elaborate and also critically scrutinise these arguments, I will analyse two cases from the Winter Olympics of 1994. These two cases are almost antithetical to each other as regards imagery, the particular staging of the performances, and the kinds of gender discourses that they seem to echo. However, beneath these differences we may find deeper similarities.

The gendering of cross-country skiing

The cultural nature of a Nordic discipline

Cross-country skiing is a Nordic discipline that may appear exotic to outside observers. It is a matter of moving efficiently through a snowy landscape, negotiating the terrain uphill, downhill and across level stretches, where skiers compete to cover a given distance in the shortest possible time. As a sports discipline, it has grown out of a long tradition of skiing as a matter of practical locomotion or means of transport in times and places where more advanced means of transportation have not been available. When this particular type of skiing was sportified around the turn of the century, it had three distinctive 'real life' roots: rural occupations, military trials and polar expeditions. Particularly in Norway, this triple heritage efficiently spanned class differences, uniting 'grassroots' and a social and cultural elite in the same activity.[13]

This unity embraced male worlds only to bring out a gender distinction more clearly: various aspects of male heroism were cemented and packed into the image of the discipline so that it took the shape of a summarising symbol (Ortner 1973). This symbolisation was also explicit on a discursive and textual level – male skiing heroism was, among other things, a common theme in pictorial art and literature.

But underneath this explicit level was a practical and experiential reality in which the difference between male and female was less clear-cut. Skiing as a source of joy and also a skill of practical importance was accessible to women, and in their upbringing girls were not as a rule discouraged from sharing in the same activities with boys.

In the history of sport, 'track and field' disciplines have generally been slow to admit women to elite competitions, and this also applies to cross-country skiing. The first Olympics at which women took part in the discipline was at Oslo in 1952. At that occasion the Norwegian representative voted against their admittance, a vote that must be seen in the light of the heavy load of male symbolism surrounding the sport in Norway. Female cross-country skiers were looked upon as an anomaly; it was commonly believed that they lacked the strength and stamina for such an arduous sport, and the toil and sweat of the track were seen as unbecoming. In other words, cross-country skiing did not fit *women*'s nature.

So, women's conquering of cross-country skiing in general, and in Norway in particular, can be described as rounds of confrontations between gatekeepers and gatecrashers. The gatekeepers grounded their standard arguments in convictions about female nature: some of them were medical experts holding convictions about the frailty of the female physique, others were sports journalists and spectators arguing from an aesthetic point of view.[14] In other words, arguments were based on the conflated conception of nature referred to above. The gatecrashers departed not only from the ongoing discourse about gender equality in society, but also from the subdued, less gender-discriminatory practices that they had experienced in their primary socialisation: the common life experience of skiing as an important cultural skill not restricted to men. In accordance with this position, gaining access to elite competitions would mean bringing sport closer to representing real life as far as gender and national culture was concerned.

The cross-country stadium: ritualisation of embodied experience

During the Winter Olympics of 1994 the cross-country stadium was crowded whether the competitors were male or female. A high proportion of the spectators were Nordic, even local, which means that they, as it were, represented the 'true owners' of the discipline. Foreign observers have drawn attention to the high proportion of children in the audience: this was clearly, for many local people, a normal family outing closely linked to a common recreational practice. Women, men and children are all supposed to share in this practice, so women competitors can be seen to complete a notion of normal 'reality', and dramatise it in Gusfield's sense.

A particularly colourful feature was the campers who braved the unusually cold weather and lived in tents in the adjoining area throughout the duration of the Games. These can be described as 'quintessential spectators' who cultivated to the extreme the experience of cold and snow that forms a tie between performers, themselves and the more ordinary native spectators. A close connection was built between spectatorship, hiking and skiing. The layout of the cross-country track is significant to this point: the main stadium where the spectators were located only exposed the skiers for a few minutes after they had started, and before they finished. Most of the track ran through a hilly woodland; it was a track through a natural landscape and recreational area. Skiing through a wintry landscape is a kinaesthetic and spatial experience that is embodied and shared by performer and part of the public. There is a merging of performer and spectator experience that is probably fuller and more specific than the identification of a universal dramatic truth suggested in Gusfield's conception of sport as drama. It is a process that can be labelled ritualisation in Bell's crucial sense quoted above, of creating a fit between body, community and cosmos as main spheres of experience (1992: 109).

However, the 'meaning' on this experiential level is not easily communicated to those who are, as it were, spectators once removed, those who only see the competition as a sportive event without sharing in the familiarity with the recreational field and a national mythology. This is one of the points at which sport as drama can be distinguished from sport as ritual participation.

At the same time, the way in which the media monitored the competitions probably added new qualities to the way different groups of spectators experienced the events either as ritual or drama. If it is a characteristic of the major sports event that it is thoroughly penetrated by the media gaze, this was especially true here. Giant TV screens and commentators kept the spectators in the stadium informed about the situation at critical points along the track, and the public address speaker frequently broke in and directed the cheering, so that the voice of the audience could not be separated from that of the loudspeaker. These Games have also been described as a friendly occasion at which an enthusiastic public hailed the champions regardless of their nationality, and this public response was certainly media-enhanced. Another interesting point is the extra effort that was made to present the women skiers as individuals before they started. After each athlete's voice was heard saying 'Hello, my name is . . . and I come from . . . ' in her own language, or in a newly learnt Norwegian phrase, she was sent onto the track accompanied by a passage of lively music. Several messages can emerge from this – that women cross-country skiers are important persons who deserve attention, and that each one of them deserves attention as contributor to the boundary-breaking Olympic event. A normal athletic category has been created where some decades ago there was nothing. And the athletes acquire individuality in the eyes of the public – something that is enlarged and further developed when the winners are publicly celebrated, as we shall see in the next section.

Winner images: ritual confirmation and symbolic spin-off

The celebration of the champions takes essentially two forms. First, there is the medal ceremony at the end of each day that sums up the days' competitions in different disciplines. This is a ritual in the conventional sense: it is highly stylised and follows a fixed agenda, and in this ceremony, the athlete's image is both enlarged and impoverished at the same time: the person is made into a national symbol, but there is no space for performance, hardly any space for the expression of individuality.

Press, radio, and TV reports present the images in different ways: sometimes distorted or even caricatured, sometimes with a serious effort to be 'true' and balanced, but always with space for individual features. These more individualised, media-created images form a varied symbolic spin-off that is open to interpretation from different angles. On this level, they differ from the stylised images created in the peak ceremonies. But on another level they retain a similarity: thanks to the media, and in particular the TV screen, the more individualised images are also magnified, and still stereotyped to a degree. This is exactly how they retain a high degree of symbolic efficiency – they are 'good to think with', and can act as spearheads in the creation of new meaning.

This is exactly how a Norwegian public was given a chance to elaborate on their preconceived notion of women skiers. Russia's Ljubov Jegorova and Italy's Manuela di Centa were the great winners of the 1994 Olympics, and their images joined those of the Norwegian models to form a more nuanced conception of what a woman cross-country skier could be like. The symbol acts in an elaborating manner (Ortner 1973), adding nuances and opening new perspectives.

Jegorova was somewhat remote in the eyes of the Norwegian public before the Games – she was known as a fabulous skier, but she was not very distinct as a person. After she had appeared in the daily TV programme that presented the winners, the press stressed her sweetness, and points were made of the fact that she enjoyed knitting. But her image remained demure and a little solemn. Di Centa's image came across as one of cheerful, extrovert and glamorous femininity. She performed this particular role for press and TV, which expressed one of her gendered identities. It could have been part of a conscious effort to counterbalance the other identity, that of an anomalous woman skier. She may have needed such a counterbalance to meet the public in her own country, being among the very first Italian female cross-country skiers to enter the world elite.

Di Centa's self-presentation contrasts to that common among Norwegian cross-country skiers: they have mostly adopted other strategies in their struggle for approval. Even if, in a media-ridden age, it is an advantage to be good-looking in addition to being a good skier, Norwegian sportswomen are usually careful not to play too openly on glamour. This is in accordance with more unisex attitudes to childrearing and a relative downplay of male–female oppositions in everyday social interaction.

On the level of gender symbolisation we are met with a repertoire of images that are all easily recognisable as they tie in with different facets of a complex gender discourse in modern society. Di Centa's glamorous and Jegorova's more homely image expose two different aspects of femininity that are widely celebrated, while the Norwegian image of a sportswoman has been modelled more according to unisex ideals. The two winner images are there as evidence available to all, but they may be perceived and interpreted in different ways. Some may read national character into the two images, interpreting them as typically Italian and Russian forms of femininity. Others again may see them as two sides of a generalised and ideal femininity. And yet another reading may see them as options for role modelling by aspiring younger sportswomen. A young Norwegian recruit is confronted with a more varied gallery of models than those of her own country, but will she emulate them or combine elements from them in *bricoleur* fashion? This brings us back to the level of embodied experience: role modelling will have to strike a balance that tunes in with the tacit layers of each local tradition, layers that are hard to change because they are acquired early in primary socialisation, consist of specific orientations in physical space, and are specific configurations of sociality, or relational modes.

We shall now leave the details of subtle variations within one discipline, and look at another discipline that exhibits a radically different gender image.

The fairy-tale of figure skating

Figure skating is a discipline in which conventional gender images are dramatised as an explicit aspect of the performance. It also brings sex-gender complementarity directly into the arena, as one of its sub-disciplines is ice dance performed by a man/woman couple. In the purely female competitions the female aesthetic is cultivated to the extreme. According to the view of Abigail Feder cited above (1995: 23) this may be a strategy to symbolically ensure the difference between the sexes in a sport in which the actual performances of men and women are very similar. Like acrobatics, figure skating favours the lightness and flexibility of youth above the strength and perseverance of adulthood, and is in this respect almost an antithesis of cross-country skiing. While many cross-country skiers achieve their best results after the age of thirty, many figure skating champions are in their teens, and the staging of the competitions also signals dependence and vulnerability, particularly in women athletes.

As we move from the cross-country stadium to the figure skating arena, we also move from a situation of shared outdoor experience to one more closely reminiscent of pure spectatorship and scenic performance. The ice hall at Hamar,[15] where the women's free-skating competition took place, is an indoor amphitheatre with a seated public, and the centrally placed rink is the scene of performance. The performance is steeped in the aesthetic and trappings associated with ballet and opera. The athlete is maximally exposed in a solo performance, and dressed in a ballet-like costume that exposes arms, legs and neck. After the performance the athlete, still in the face of the public, joins the coach and waits anxiously for the results, and the suspense is released in an emotional reaction and hugs of joy or comfort visible to all. A family-like and personal element is brought out, evoking a notion of the athlete as youthful and dependent. The compact and theatre-like arrangement of the rink creates an impression of a back-stage (Goffman 1959) brought to the front.

Mythical themes

The women's free-skating in the 1994 Olympics was an event at which several mythical themes were worked through. The three main charac-ters of the plot were the two American skaters, Tonya Harding and Nancy Kerrigan, and sixteen-year-old Oksana Baiul from Ukraine, who won the gold medal. There were moving features in Oksana's life story. She was a orphan from a poor background, and came from a country which was currently at a dramatic historical crossroads. Harding and Kerrigan attracted an immense amount of attention before and during the games because of the jealousy and conflict between them, drummed up by American media into a true soap opera. The prologue was an attack on Nancy Kerrigan earlier in the season, when her leg was slashed. Tonya Harding was believed to have staged this attack, and for some time it was doubtful whether either of them would make it to the Games – Kerrigan because of the injury, and Harding because of the suspicion against her. At the final competition numerous Americans in the audience expressed their sympathies very clearly. There were banners with slogans like 'Go home, Tonya' and 'We Love Nancy'. Tonya Harding's performance was beset with tension and misfortune, and she ended up placed eighth. Nancy Kerrigan won the silver medal, to the disappointment of her supporters who had hoped that she would win the competition.

In his analysis of sport as drama, Gusfield mentions the 'David and Goliath' myth as one popular theme that is sometimes the outcome of a sports competition: the unknown guy wins over the famous guy. The romantic setting of figure skating brings in other stories, ones more directly linked to ballet, opera and movies.[16] The women's free-skating in 1994 was partly beset with the theme of Beauty and the Beast. The outcome of the competition was more than anything a Cinderella story, and even the Ugly Sisters can be glimpsed in the background.

The notion of vulnerability was woven into the myths about the athletes and given a distinctly moral twist in the ongoing comments on Nancy Kerrigan's leg injury for which Tonya Harding was blamed, and Harding's bad luck was partly interpreted as deserved punishment for her alleged attack on Nancy Kerrigan.

Towards some analytical lessons

It is now time to go back to the outset and reconsider the questions that were posed there: is there such a thing as a global ritual, can an athletic competition be seen as such a ritual, and how widely can symbols be shared? These were admittedly intended as rather rhetorical questions, since it has been my major concern to argue that all these issues have to be broken down further into more specific ones. I shall now reconsider the more specific questions as they have been high-lighted through the discussion of the case material.

Ritual, drama or spectacle: a matter of positioning

Both cross-country and figure skating competitions are spectacular events at which colourful imagery is exhibited. Yet there are important differences in the ways in which the spectators' roles and experience are orchestrated in the two events.

At the cross-country stadium spectatorship for some is turned into an active ritual participation. The commentator becomes a ritual priest who directs the cheering, which in its turn becomes a wave[17] of collective encouragement meant to spur the athlete along. To part of the audience, presence in the stadium was in tune with an embodied cultural experience of hiking and enjoying nature. The track itself runs through a natural landscape; some spectators had made their way there on their own skis, some even camped in the forest for several days and nights during the Games. The efforts of the competitive skiers are a kind of experience that the spectators themselves can share, albeit on a vastly more modest level. There is a clear continuity between the sport and some celebrated features of Norwegian recreational activities – at least in people's perceptions. The continuity is sealed in ritualised presence and serious participation in the stadium. At the same time, the full content of this ritual event becomes rather esoteric and inaccessible to outsiders who lack this kind of contextual experience. True, as stated above, there is also a great deal of explicit symbolic – even textual – material, but this too is rather inaccessible to an international public.

To all spectators, the event is both drama and spectacle. It is a dramatic (in Gusfield's sense) competition between athletes who carry specific meanings to the spectators. It is also a spectacular event opening up for a free flow of symbolic elaboration.

The figure skating event differs in many ways. The relationship of the public to the athletes is different: here is a seated public admiring a stage show that has the trappings of ballet, opera and fairy-tale. Unlike cross-country skiing, the reference material consists of mythological, textual and scenic traditions that are widely known by a western public. In comparison, the textual material of cross-country skiing is more restricted to a Nordic public. And, in further contrast to the cross-country event, there are probably very few among the figure skating audience that have ever had an embodied experience akin to what the skaters do. The skiers engage in a sport that many of the devoted spectators can emulate to some degree, but the figure skaters perform an art that takes years of training to achieve. On the other hand, the figure skating event is much more like a drama that seems to tell a 'true life' story. The focus on the athletes and the people on whom they depend heightens this effect: I can think of no other sport that exhibits such a close-up, visible backstage. All taken together, drama and performativity seem to overshadow the component of ritualisation if we focus on the experiential quality of spectatorship. An immense amount of symbolic spin-off is created, and interpretations of this are steered into specific veins by the theatrical trappings and widely recognisable mythic allusions. But this ritual identification does not rest on the same experiential fundament as that of the native skiing public. It most probably rests on precarious and moralist gender values: that good and deserving girls should be rewarded.

Ritual or ritualised activity is found as bounded sequences within the Olympic spectacle. Any sports contest has its ritual agenda that takes care of fairness and the purity of competitor categories. In the case material presented here, the contests take on a dimension of ritual commitment for some spectators, but not for all – or at least, not in the same way for all. What is a deeply felt commitment to some, may be just an enjoyable – or perhaps even silly – performance to others. This implies that one and the same event may take on different characteristics to different onlookers – if by ritualisation we imply involvement, duty and faith, what is performance to some can be a ritual to others.

Embodied experience and symbolic spin-off: two levels of orientation

We can take a sportive event and discover new topics to be ritualised, and new twists to the truths that are to be celebrated. At the cross-country arena it was the superb female skier who was celebrated – perhaps we can, in a bold and imaginative leap, suggest that for a moment nationalistic pride was suspended, and the embodied experience linked to the sport was alloyed to a feeling of global identification; in other words, the ritualised linking between body, cosmos and community (Bell 1992: 109) was transposed from a national to a global level. 'Global ritual' may be an unmanageable concept, yet here we have a situation in which a locally based public went through a ritual experience that possibly strengthened their *global* self-identification.

The figure skating event gave rise to a powerful series of analogies, elaborated by the media, between Oksana Baiul's hardships, youth and vulnerability on the one hand and the hardships, youth and vulnerability of the former Soviet republic as a sovereign nation state on the other. In this case a more explicit production of metaphors transposed the meaning from 'orphan Cinderella' to 'symbol of a new political future'.

In the cross-country instance, embodied experience was affected by the presence of the media in the arena. In the figure skating instance, an athlete's body was seen as a symbol in a chain of metaphoric creations that make sense within a repertoire of discursive meaning shared by a western public.

Ritual and performativity have been linked to embodied experience and symbolic traffic respectively, and have been treated as analytically distinguishable processes. Yet they are interdependent. Just as there is a traffic of symbolic material – in this case images of persons – horizontally across various social and even national boundaries, there is also a vertical traffic between levels of experience. Symbols created through the clever marriage of performance and media technique may penetrate to the deeper layers of ritual identification and modify them, as in the possible transposition from a national to a global communal and cosmological level.

Making persons

The idea that ritual makes persons lies close at hand, and extends far beyond its roots in the work of Van Gennep and Turner on rites of passage. In a more extended sense it is clearly expressed in Bell (1992: 21) and Hughes-Freeland (1998: 10). The analysis undertaken in this chapter suggests two levels of person making, corresponding to the main distinction between ritual embodiment on the one hand, and symbolic creativity on the other.

The first level concerns the way in which ritualised action shapes dispositions. A processual view of ritual as a genre of social action (Bell 1992; Humphrey and Laidlaw 1994) enables us to pinpoint crucial connections between ritual involvement and the internalisation of basic values in the social actor.

On the second level, the performative and dramatic aspects of sport and its representation in the media create overly clear and simplified person images that are 'good to think with', and lend themselves easily to production of meaning. This is visible in the lively creation of metaphors arising from the figure skating event, as well as in the more restricted way in which the cross-country champions of the 1994 Games enriched the Norwegian conception of the female skier. It remains to be seen whether these new images of the female skier are able – through symbolic traffic between experiential levels – to make their way back to the embodied level via emulation and role modelling in an enlarged 'room' of cultural reproduction.

Postscript: does sport offer a 'final truth' about gender?

Persons are gendered, and gender messages and gender 'truths' are embedded in the rituals and symbol-production of the sports contest. In my introduction I suggested that variation might hide some common messages, and that sport speaks particularly clearly about gender difference and equality.

Gender-wise, the two disciplines analysed here seem to emit two different series of messages. Cross-country skiing mirrors the contemporary equalisation in society at large. Its imagery opens up and becomes more varied, it creates new options and develops an athletic category until it has taken on a complexity that emulates the complexity of real-life role repertoires. The athletes are adult individuals in their own right. If Di Centa is glamorous, she is also pointedly adult and self-sufficient as a person.

Figure skating cultivates the romantic and the sentimental. The symbolic complexity that it creates cultivates mythic prototypes, and symbolic redundancy towards maintaining an image of conventional hyper-femininity.

Are we, then, confronted with a movement towards multivocality, or towards 'final truths'? No symbols 'mean' in any specific way. Conversely, some uncontested truths that are celebrated in ritual but not necessarily phrased as explicit principles, may, as occasion arises, be pulled to the front and made the focus of explicit discourse. This can, for instance, happen to the celebration of the 'natural human being' which lies at the core of sport and has a dubious status in modern gender discourses. The biological final sorting principle which assures that competitions must always be restricted to pure sexual categories, signals the importance of biology over culture, and is at odds with gender neutralising processes at work in other areas of societal life. Which one will win in the final round? Discussions about the genesis of human qualities, gender roles and gender habitus included, tends to oscillate between a 'genetic' and a 'cultural' view. The genetic view seems to be on the rise now, and if that is so, sport – be it cross-country skiing, figure skating or any other discipline – may deliver powerful 'truths' about 'natural' gender difference.

Notes

1 In a separate work, I utilise partly overlapping case material to give a broader analysis of how gender discourses in sport articulate with those of 'society at large' (Rudie, in press). In that work the issue of ritual and performativity, although briefly touched upon, is left undeveloped.

2 For instance, it is essential to be careful about the distinction between 'meaning for someone' and 'meaning in itself' (see Shore 1996).

3 It is of course important not to confuse equality and sameness (see Gullestad 1986, 1989). However, as males are expected to outperform women on biological grounds in most sports, and in fact mostly do, this difference may nourish a suspicion that claims of equality in other areas are unrealistic. I have followed up this argument in more detail (Rudie, in press).

4 Pierre de Coubertin, who revitalised the Olympic Games in 1894, saw the combined cultivation of national character and international understanding as a positive force. This was to be achieved through competition within both athletic and artistic fields of excellence.

5 '[Ethnic and cultural] fragmentation and modernist homogenisation are not two arguments, two opposing views of what is happening in the world today, but two constitutive trends of global reality' (Friedman 1994: 102).

6 My study forms part of a cooperative project with five other anthropologists; each of us focused on different aspects of the Games. Professor A. M. Klausen was initiator and leader of the joint project. Among the publications by group members are: Klausen *et al.* 1995; Klausen 1996; Klausen (ed.) in press. Works by individual team members are quoted separately in the main text.

7 A good example of this can be found in Norwegian skiers of the first decades of this century. In particular, the champions in the Nordic disciplines (jumping and cross-country skiing) often came from rural backgrounds, worked in rural occupations, and were self-coached.

8 Connerton (1989) explores the distinction between inscribing and incorporating practices, and argues for the importance of the latter – together with commemorating ceremonies – as a store of social memory and hence a stabilising force in social processes.

9 See Bourdieu 1977; Lakoff 1987; Johnson 1987; Connerton 1989; Taussig 1993; Strathern 1996.

10 This does not, of course, amount to saying that the meanings attached to various sports, or the complete reading of the activities, are the same against all cultural traditions.

11 Berkaak (in press) draws attention to how the expression 'mega event' emerged in the discourse around the 1994 Olympics during the period of preparation.

12 I have explored this argument in greater detail elsewhere (Rudie, in press).

13 This has been explored in Christensen 1993 and Klausen *et al.* 1995.

14 Ingrid Wigernæs, a pioneer cross-country skier and later coach during a decisive period from the mid-1950s to the late 1960s, has described this in her book (Wigernæs 1968).

15 The speed skating and figure skating competitions took place at Hamar, about sixty kilometres from Lillehammer.

16 After having worked for some time on my material, I became acquainted with Baughman's (1995) edited volume. I found many of my own interpretations paralleled in this volume, which may be read as a more complete story, and one told from a more consistently feminist perspective.

17 'The Wave' was itself a spectacular feature of the 1994 Winter Olymics, and it was rehearsed in advance. To my knowledge it was launched on the first TV show transmitted during the torch relay. It was an orchestrated gesture of applause consisting of a movement of raised hands through a crowd, starting at one end of an arena and making its way towards the other.

Bibliography

Baughman, C. (ed.) (1995) *Women on Ice: Feminist Essays on the Tonya Harding/Nancy Kerrigan Spectacle*, New York and London: Routledge.

Bell, C. (1992) *Ritual Theory, Ritual Practice*, New York and Oxford: Oxford University Press.

Berkaak, O. A. (in press) ' "In the Heart of the Volcano": The Olympic Games as Modern Megadrama', in A. M. Klausen (ed.) *Olympic Games as Performance and Public Event*, Oxford: Berghahn Books.

Bourdieu, P. (1977) *Outline of a Theory of Practice*, Cambridge and New York: Cambridge University Press.

Christensen, O. (1993) *Skiidrett før Sondre*, Oslo: Ad notam Gyldendal.

Connerton, P. (1989) *How Societies Remember*, Cambridge: Cambridge University Press.

Csordas, T. J. (ed.) (1994) *Embodiment and Experience: The Existential Ground of Culture and Self*, Cambridge: Cambridge University Press.

Feder, A. M. (1995) ' "A Radiant Smile from the Lovely Lady": Overdetermined Femininity in "Ladies' " Figure Skating', in C. Baughman (ed.) *Women on Ice: Feminist Essays on the Tonya Harding/Nancy Kerrigan Spectacle*, New York and London: Routledge.

Friedman, J. (1994) *Cultural Identity and Global Process*, London: Sage.

Goffman, E. (1959) *The Presentation of Self in Everyday Life*, Harmondsworth: Penguin.

Gusfield, J. (1987) 'Sports as Story: Content and Form in Agonistic Games', in Kang Shinpyo, J. MacAloon and R. DaMatta (eds) *The Olympics and Cultural Exchange*, Korea: Institute for Ethnological Studies, Hanyang University.

Gullestad, M. (1986) 'Symbolic fences in urban Norwegian neighbourhoods', *Ethnos*, 51, 1–2: 52–69.

—— (1989) *Kultur og Hevrdagsliv*, Oslo: Universitetsforlaget.

Hoberman, J. (1992) *Mortal Engines: The Science of Performance and the Dehumanization of Sport*, New York: The Free Press.

Hughes-Freeland, F. (ed.) (1998) *Ritual, Performance, Media*, London and New York: Routledge.

Humphrey, C. and Laidlaw, J. (1994) *The Archetypal Actions of Ritual*, Oxford: Clarendon Press.

Johnson, M. (1987) *The Body in the Mind: The Bodily Basis of Meaning, Imagination, and Reason*, Chicago IL: University of Chicago Press.

Klausen, A. M. (1996) *Lillehammer og Olympismen*, Oslo: Ad notam Gyldendal.

Klausen, A. M., Berkaak, O. A., Aslaksen, E., Puijk, R., Rudie, I. and Archetti, E. (1995) *Fakkelstafetten: En Olympisk Ouverture*, Oslo: Ad notam Gyldendal.

Klausen, A. M. (ed.) (in press) *Olympic Games as Performance and Public Event*, Oxford: Berghahn Books.

Lakoff, G. (1987) *Women, Fire, and Dangerous Things: What Categories Reveal about the Mind*, Chicago IL and London: University of Chicago Press.

MacAloon, J. (1984) 'Olympic Games and the Theory of Spectacle in Modern Societies', in J. MacAloon (ed.) *Rite, Drama, Festival, Spectacle: Rehearsals*

Toward a Theory of Cultural Performance, Philadelphia PA: Institute for the Study of Human Issues.

Ortner, S. (1973) 'On Key Symbols', *American Anthropologist*, 75: 1338–46.

Puijk, R. (in press) 'Producing Norwegian Culture for Domestic and Foreign Gazes: The Lillehammer Olympic Opening Ceremony', in A. M. Klausen (ed.) *Olympic Games as Performance and Public Event*, Oxford: Berghahn Books.

Rostas, S. (1998) 'From Ritualisation to Performativity: The Concheros of Mexico', in F. Hughes-Freeland (ed.) *Ritual, Performance, Media*, ASA monograph 35, London and New York: Routledge.

Rudie, I. (in press) 'Equality, Hierarchy and Pure Categories: Gender Images in the Winter Olympics', in A. M. Klausen (ed.) *Olympic Games as Performance and Public Event*, Oxford: Berghahn Books.

Shore, B. (1996) *Culture in Mind*, New York: Oxford University Press.

Strathern, A. J. (1996) *Body Thoughts*, Ann Arbor MI: University of Michigan Press.

Taussig, M. (1993) *Mimesis and Alterity: A Particular History of the Senses*, New York and London: Routledge.

Turner, V. (1986) *The Anthropology of Performance*, New York: PAJ Publications.

Van Gennep, A. (1960) [1909] *The Rites of Passage*, translated by M.B. Wizedom and G.L. Caffee, Chicago: University of Chicago Press.

Wigernæs, I. (1968) *Mot mål med Jentutn*, Oslo: Aschehoug.

Chapter 7

Reimagining identity, cultural production and locality under transnationalism

Performances of *San Juan* in the Ecuadorean Andes

Mary M. Crain

We live in a mass-mediated world characterised by conditions of elec-tronic propinquity as well as transnational flows of populations, ideas, images and commodities.[1] Acknowledging the contemporary cultural ecumene, some of the recent theorising in social anthropology argues that culture can no longer be mapped with place.[2] In such an intercon-nected world, we must critically evaluate one of the central gatekeeping concepts in anthropology, the notion of 'the field'. As Lavie and Swedenburg (1996: 1, 2) have argued, within the discipline of anthro-pology, the field was defined as a spatially demarcated territory where culture could be found and studied. It was distant from western metropolitan centres, where anthropologists were typically trained. Culture was located in 'the outback' or in 'the colonies', places occu-pied by 'primitive groups', tribal peoples, and later, by peasant populations. However, today 'the non-western world' has imploded into 'the western world', as people who were once 'distant others' may now live next door to us. Today, with the movements of globetrotting elites, tourists, political refugees and various diasporic groups, we are witnessing a blurring of the boundaries separating 'our home' from 'the field'.

Notions of pure, 'authentic' cultures are also being abandoned, as ethnographers realise that earlier conceptualisations of communities as bounded, self-contained entities ignored those interconnections between places which had always existed (Wolf 1982). Historical processes of colonisation and geographical displacement as well as the accelerated interaction of diverse life-worlds today, often resulting from travel and media flows, have also undermined scholarly paradigms such as that of 'a stable subject' or 'essentialised identities'. As a result of earlier influences of colonisation as well as more recent practices associated with modernity, the identities of more and more groups throughout the world are hybridised constructions which are crafted out of materials that are neither entirely local nor entirely global (Hannerz 1987; Howes 1996).[3]

What does it mean to be a member of, and a participant in, a seemingly 'local ritual community' in a transnational era? This chapter draws on my analysis of the feast day of Saint John the Baptist, a patron saint celebration which momentarily brings cosmopolitan elites as well as globally savvy indigenous peoples together, in Quimsa, a once-backroads rural community of the Ecuadorean Andes, in order to illuminate some of the methodological and representational challenges facing anthropology during the late twentieth century. During an era in which face-to-face relations in local communities are, in many instances, limited to more circumscribed contexts, examination of *San Juan* (Saint John) illustrates the manner in which different classes, ethnic groups and genders travel (Clifford 1997). Focusing on the context of the *San Juan* fiesta, Gupta and Ferguson's (1997: 4) request for 'further ethnographic research which problematises all associations between peoples, cultures, and localities' is pursued. These authors maintain that 'cultural territorialisations' can no longer (if they ever could) be considered as given, natural entities, tied to particular spatial terrains. Rather they are the result of complex, contingent historical and political processes whose construction must be explained. This chapter aims to explain the continuing appeal of *San Juan* both for particular Ecuadorean elites as well as indigenous people within a world characterised both by dispersed populations and by voluntary migration.

I present the ethnographic evidence for selecting a performative approach for the study of ritualised action. A series of vignettes illuminates the interplay of elite–indigenous relations during this three-day festive celebration. The chapter closes by examining the implications of the performative aspects of *San Juan* for issues of identity formation and place-making.

Why performance?

Recent literature on performance (Schechner and Apel 1990; Schechner 1992; Taussig 1993; Hughes-Freeland 1998) as well as ethnographic studies of cultural performance (MacAloon 1984; Schieffelin 1985; Fernandez 1986; Lavie *et al.* 1993; Myers 1994; Dubisch 1995; Crain 1996) provides an organising framework for this investigation of *San Juan*, and the group-specific claims which are articulated within this ritual frame. MacAloon (1984: 1) suggests that cultural performances are 'occasions in which as a culture we reflect upon and define ourselves, dramatise our collective myths and history, present ourselves with alternatives, and eventually change in some ways while remaining the same in others'. Adopting a more radical stance, Taussig (1993: xv) reiterates an earlier insight that 'most of what seems important in life is made up', reminding us that the distinction between 'the seemingly real' and 'artifice is a social construction'. In contrast to the classic structural-functionalist approaches to ritual as a set of collective representations which contributed to the integration of a relatively homogeneous cultural group and reproduced an unchanging tradition, a performative framework acknowledges creativity and innovation by highlighting the agency of diverse performers who, despite structural constraints, pursue strategies to construct themselves and their worlds, in relation to larger publics. My exploration of *San Juan* as a 'contemporary performance' in which indigenous people and elites engage in identity politics, moves analysis away from consensual approaches to the study of ritual in anthropology. I argue that the former patron saint ritual has been recast as a series of cultural performances in which the preceding groups advance diverse claims which affirm, negotiate, and/or challenge particular identities. But before considering the performative aspects of *San Juan* in further detail, I provide an ethnographic and historical contextualisation.

Ethnographic background

Prior to Spanish colonisation of the New World in the late fifteenth century, the autochthonous ancestors of contemporary Quimseños inhabited both the fertile valley floors as well as the hilly slopes of what is now the parish of Angochahua, province of Imbabura. From the sixteenth century through the beginning of the eighteenth century, native control over this territory diminished, as the Crown awarded both Spanish colonial families as well as religious institutions title to landed estates in Angochahua. *Indios libres* ('free indigenous communities') were displaced onto the adjacent hillsides and *indios propios* ('owned Indian communities') were given use rights to small hacienda plots for subsistence purposes. In exchange, the latter worked five to six days per week for the estates. While many of the landed elites were veteran travellers, cosmopolitans who maintained residences in Quito

and occasionally in Europe, *indios propios* were tied to landed properties by various forms of debt peonage. Their knowledge of, and travel
to other places was restricted. Hacienda La Miranda, the research site
under consideration here, was by the late eighteenth century one of
three large estates dominating the parish of Angochahua. It was the
property of the Rodríguez Laras, one of Ecuador's most renowned
landowning families.

The feast of *San Juan*, the patron saint of Quimsa, is celebrated
every 22–24 June. Instead of stamping out all forms of paganism and
idolatry in the New World during the early colonial period, Spanish
priests frequently superimposed Catholic religious holidays, such as
that of *San Juan* which honors the birth of St John the Baptist, to
dovetail roughly with pre-Hispanic periods of native feasting.[4] Buitrón
comments:

> although the true origin of *San Juan* is not known there is no
> doubt that the Indians held celebrations at approximately this time
> long before the arrival of the Spaniards in the New World. The
> chroniclers spoke of a grand indigenous festival that took place
> during the summer solstice. It could be that the actual festival of
> *San Juan* is the ancient festival of the sun.
>
> (1964: 168)

Catholicism played an important role in the legitimisation of the hierarchical agrarian class relations throughout highland Ecuador. The
haciendas, owned both by private families as well as by religious orders,
served as centres of religious instruction for their labour force. Most
owned small chapels and estate owners paid for the services of itinerant
priests. Elite largesse was demonstrated through calendrical rites, the
most important of which was the celebration of the patron saint of *San
Juan*, which estate owners such as the Rodríguez family co-sponsored
with the peasantry. Religion was incorporated as a disciplinary feature
of everyday life. The indigenous peasantry rose at five o'clock every
morning for *las rezas* (public prayers), performed under the guidance
of resident nuns in the hacienda courtyard, before beginning the
working day. The Catholic church also sought lay indigenous leaders
to fulfil minor ecclesiastical roles at community level, such as that of *el
prioste* (ritual sponsor).

Although hacienda chapels served by Catholic priests were accessible to indigenous peasants, the peasantry also adhered to alternative
cosmologies and ceremonial rites which were unique to them, such as

nature worship, in which they harnessed the sacred powers of the land-scape. For example, they venerated spirits residing on the mountain tops, believed in the reproductive power of *cuichi* (the rainbow) and also pursued traditions of healing (Crain 1991). Both in the past and in the present, such unofficial practices have differentiated them from the much smaller community of landowners as well as their *mestizo* employees (persons of mixed descent, both Hispanic and indigenous) who pursued more orthodox forms of Catholicism. Local Catholicism as it took root in the native communities was 'Andeanised', combining certain pre-Hispanic beliefs and practices with other Christian views (Eade and Sallnow 1991).

It was not until the 1950s that mounting demographic pressure prompted public debates regarding the abolition of servile labour in the Ecuadorean highlands. Many Angochahuan estate owners feared that their entire properties would be subject to state expropriation and distributed to peasant cooperatives. It was at this point, perhaps as a pre-emptive strategy to deter peasant mobilisation from below, that Señor Rodríguez enacted his 'own private agrarian reform' in 1962, two years before the national reform. His reform absolved obligatory labour service, instituted wage labour and redistributed subsistence plots to many peasant families. Attempting to reduce any future demands for a more equitable land redistribution programme 'at home', Señor Rodríguez promoted various migratory strategies during the 1960s to secure employment for *indígenas* (the new self-definition adopted by the former *indios propios* of the hacienda) in a wide range of outposts such as the national capital Quito, Caracas, Venezuela and Washington DC – sites where he had familial and business ties. His initiative stimulated the first widespread emigration from the community (Crain 1996).[5]

Today the community of Quimsa, an ethnically mixed, un-nucleated settlement of some two thousand indigenous and mestizo peasants and artisans, lies immediately beyond the stone walls of the Hacienda La Miranda. Although it is located some two hours by public transport from Quito, Quimsa is a dormitory community, and thus forms an integral part of this cosmopolitan centre. Although these figures vary somewhat by season, approximately 40–50 per cent of the economi-cally active members of all Quimsa households, those men and women whose earnings help to underwrite the village economy, work outside of Quimsa. They return to spend their weekends, to vote in commu-nity assemblies and to participate in fiestas, the most famous of which is *San Juan*, whereas during weekdays, senior women, the elderly and children predominate in village life.[6]

While *indígenas* are perceived to be the primary protagonists of *San Juan*, the Rodríguez elites have also been loyal in their role as co-sponsors of this event. They celebrate both with *indígenas* as well as with members of their extended family at the Hacienda La Miranda on the third day of *San Juan*. In contrast, most of the other estate owners in the parish now refuse to participate in the elaborate rituals associated with the pre-agrarian reform period, many of which were characterised by transgressive behaviour, framed against the backdrop of the colourful pageantry of 'Indianness'. The latter complain that such rituals, particularly *San Juan*, are a drain on their profits, interrupt production schedules and are potentially violent. In contrast to the preceding landowners, the Rodríguez elites are more influential actors at the national level and they also move in much more global circles. By participating with *indígenas* in *San Juan*, members of the Rodríguez family are praised by some elites as conservationists of an otherwise disappearing cultural tradition, while criticised by others as decadent supporters of the *ancien régime* who have betrayed the common economic interests of today's commercial farmers. However, the current co-sponsorship of the Rodríguez family during *San Juan* cannot readily be attributed to economic factors. Their contemporary involvement in this event is best comprehended in light of their symbolic efforts to appropriate the power and signs of 'Indianness' as a part of their new global construction of selfhood. The Rodríguez elites' identities have been reconfigured in light of a late twentieth-century sign-economy, with its accompanying search for unique representations that emphasise 'difference' and novelty. In many European arenas which these elites frequent, diverse publics want to be Indian. Romanticised images of 'Andean Indianness' circulate which laud indigenous panpipe music and portray *indígenas* as both closer to nature, and as the producers of homespun, artisanal goods that are superior in quality to mass-produced commodities.

In what follows, I provide accounts of several *San Juan* performances as they unfolded chronologically. These accounts constitute my own attempt to evoke particular perceptions of *San Juan* as I experienced it, on several different occasions over the course of a ten-year period, ranging from my fieldwork in June 1982, through June 1983, and finally during June 1992, and are followed in each case by a commentary. The first vignette focuses primarily on relations between a heterogeneous group of indigenous peoples, both residents of the community of Quimsa and migrants originally born in Quimsa who return for *San Juan*. The second vignette occurs on 24 June within the courtyard of the Hacienda La Miranda, and attends to intercultural interactions between indigenous peoples, members of the Rodríguez family and a varied audience of spectators. The third vignette analyses performances unfolding during an offstage ritual held by elites for other elites on 24 June, the climax of this three-day celebration.

Vignette one

For Quimseños, *San Juan* festivities begin on the first evening, of 22 June, and continue through the following day. They occur on Indian terrain in *El Alto* (Upper Quimsa), away from any direct surveillance of the Rodríguez elites. *El Alto* is the local term used to designate the bulk of the territory allocated to the indigenous community following the 1962 agrarian reform. By the afternoon of 22 June 1982, residents' homes have been cleaned and polished, and many other houses, which have been abandoned for much of the year, are thrown open to the light of day and floors are swept to await *el retorno* (the return). Several hours later, a number of buses, either from Quito or from the provincial capital and overloaded with the grown children of Quimsa villagers, crawl along the one-lane cobblestone road that leads towards the village. Upon arrival, passengers descend toting plastic bags full of new hats, shawls, scarves, guitars and boom boxes, as well as money for their parents and other kin who reside in the community on a more permanent basis. A few of 'the new arrivals' impress their long-lost neighbours by hiring taxis in the provincial capital to deliver them to their doorstep. The most extravagant members of this crowd have journeyed by plane, coming from as far afield as Washington DC and Caracas, Venezuela. By 7.30 p.m. mass is held inside the hacienda chapel. Those Quimseños who attend the ceremony make a hasty exit in order to return to *El Alto*. It is here that many of 'the new arrivals', particularly the male participants, 'become Indians' overnight. The men shed their western apparel, consisting of made-in-Taiwan polyester clothing, and replace it with indigenous ritual dress which has either been kept for them or loaned to them by their Quimsa-based relatives. Female migrants, who wear Indian-style clothing outside the community, frequently *estrenar* (show off for the first time) an outfit especially made for this occasion. In *El Alto* male ritual players don masks and other disguises typical of *San Juan*. Ritual sponsors organise *cuadrillas* (dancing teams), with their *compadres* (co-godparents).

Each *cuadrilla* navigates its way through the corn fields, visiting from door to door.

Accompanying a *prioste* on the first evening, I entered the first adobe home. We were greeted in topsy-turvy manner with a chorus of *buenos dias* (good day), even though the sky was dark, as it was nine o'clock in the evening. A makeshift altar, fashioned of straw and adorned with *un santo* (a wooden image of St John) occupied a prominent place in what was typically the only room.[7] Both saint and altar were decorated with Ecuadorean currency, US dollar bills, homemade bread dolls, pineapples, bananas, bottles of *aguardiente* (cane liquor) as well as family photographs. Upon entry, we exchanged greetings with our hosts and our *prioste* group began various rounds of contra-dancing accompanied by *san juanitos* (songs typically sung by all dancers during *San Juan* to honor the saint). These were punctuated by drinks of *chicha* (maize beer) and *aguardiente* awarded to us by our hosts in return for our laborious dancing efforts. In 1982 and 1983 it was not unusual to see Quimseños using tape recorders to document their performances, and by 1992 camcorders were also in evidence.

In addition to the household members, two different bands composed of indigenous musicians were present. The first were members of the internationally renowned band Boliviamanta, who had travelled to Quimsa for the first time in 1992 to demonstrate pan-Andean solidarity with their ethnic brothers and sisters. These musicians were friends of *indígenas* in Quimsa who had invited them to participate in *San Juan*, but there was no payment or sponsorship involved. Boliviamanta had recently arrived from La Paz toting a copy of their new album just released in France. The second band, Ñanda Manachi, was composed of several Quimseños who had also just returned from Bolivia. There they had re-established ties with Boliviamanta and were introduced to a Dutch agent regarding the production of their second album. Other more 'locally based' Quimseños moved around with recorders, taping the music while simultaneously pursuing their own Indian-style dance steps.

A Parisian man with a slick-backed ponytail, whom I later discovered had been the French promoter of Boliviamanta's album, was also present. He was drinking heavily and trying to imitate the dance sequences of a team of Indian men. 'Urban Indians', born in Quimsa, who had momentarily abandoned their city lives as construction workers, domestic servants and cafeteria waitresses in Quito, also made an appearance. They were accompanied by two young Indian men from the neighbouring community of Otavalo, one of whom sported an elaborate earring which generated a great deal of commentary among the indigenous elders. Finally, during 1983, three indigenous women displayed the most coveted prestige item of the season: woollen shawls of vibrant colours. Imported from Czechoslovakia, these shawls are a recent component of Indian women's ritual wardrobe. Unavailable in Ecuador, they may only be obtained from Macy's or other large department stores in the United States. Their procurement depends on purchase by indigenous relatives, who are members of a community of diasporic Quimseños residing in Washington DC.

San Juan constitutes a period of licence for Quimsa Indians, in which the codes structuring everyday life and work routines are inverted and elite behavior is parodied. Masks are often worn, and many male *indígenas* dress as *blancos* (white people), enacting roles such as the hacienda owner, *el mayordomo* (the whip-cracking overseer of the pre-agrarian reform hacienda), the national politician, the military officer and the priest. Other popular disguises include *el payaso* (the clown) and the devil. For example, in the dwellings which I entered, many of the Indian men paraded in masquerade. Some made a caricature of authority figures by portraying them as buffoons. A few men had put on long frocks, or lengthened a wife's petticoat in order to imitate a priest's robe. Another man wore a national military uniform which he had put on backwards. He combined this with a floppy straw hat commonly purchased by foreign tourists, huge Ray-Ban sunglasses, and a limp replica of the Ecuadorean flag that he waved around flamboyantly. Others appeared in masks painted with 'facial features of whites which included blonde hair, blue eyes and mustaches' (Crespi 1981: 492). While masquerade is typically associ-ated with indigenous performances of *San Juan*, it is not a static tradition and has always been subject to creative innovation.[8] For example, during June 1983, improvised elements culled from urban popular culture, such as a facial mask of Ronald Reagan, were combined with other items corresponding to the more traditional *mayordomo* outfit. Similarly, *the dia-uma* (devil's head) mask, a disguise characteristic of the *San Juan* fiesta in the indigenous community of Atahualpa, some ten kilometres to the north, was also in evidence in June 1983. And similar to other ritual inversions, gender and sexual ambiguities were highlighted during *San Juan*. Indigenous men engaged in transvestism by donning female garments such as petticoats and *centros* (elaborate pleated skirts) and by accentuating female bodily attributes and gestures. Several men who cross-dressed appropriated the reproductive power of indigenous women. They often carried a doll in their shawls which resembled an infant, and had swollen bellies indicative of pregnancy.

Commentary on vignette one

In *El Alto* indigenous performances often express symbolic opposition to the dominant culture, including Catholic orthodoxy. *Indígenas* have shaped this cult of a Catholic saint to foreground carnivalesque dimensions that accentuate the playful irreverence of masquerade. Quimseños brazenly embrace identities which mock the elite construction of self, just as their performative behaviour confuses those boundaries normally separating high culture from low culture. For example, those who wear military uniforms in an irreverent style reverse the identities of the nation state and draw attention to their own emergent ethnic identities instead. Through subversive practices of mimesis they acquire the power of the signs associated with the dominant culture for themselves (Taussig 1993; Kane 1994).

By participating in this rite, Quimseños assert their identity to themselves and *vis-à-vis* a larger world. A contemporary celebration of cultural difference that contains an important pre-Hispanic substrate, St John is referred to as 'the Indian saint'. Native support for this cult now exists independently of support from either the parish church, other ecclesiastical authorities or the landed elite. As Taylor (1982: 305) has argued for the carnaval *sambistas* (samba dance troupes) of Rio de Janeiro's *favelas* (shanty towns), Quimseños 'live for San Juan', and their social identities are shaped by the forms of communal association that this event engenders.

The incorporation of different forms of imported media technology often associated with diverse cultural modernities, as recent components of *San Juan*, has revitalised this tradition, frequently by expanding audience participation. For example, taped cassettes of *san juanitos* as well as videotapes of the feast day, are loaned to any Quimseño or other interested party who could not be present. Similarly, re-runs of videotaped performances of *San Juan* are frequently viewed in Quimsa, particularly during the weekends when community residents have more free time and those Quimseños who work in Quito are back 'home'. Community residents enjoy commenting on these re-runs in large groups, either in the home of someone who owns a videotape player or in Quimsa's Communal House. These videos are favoured over many of the foreign programmes, such as *Star Trek*, which are broadcast on national television. Furthermore, video documentation during *San Juan* of bands such as Boliviamanta and Ñanda Manachi, who have gained a transnational *cachet* by being labelled 'world music' as well as 'Andean folk music', makes powerful statements about shifting cosmopolitan tastes and transnational identities while simultaneously fomenting a sense of cultural and ethnic identity among Quimseños.

Indigenous cultural performances enacted during *San Juan* which display ceremonial dress codes as well as dance traditions which elites perceive to be 'authentic', have become valuable signs of what it means to be a Quimseño *indígena* in social settings which are primarily organised by non-indigenous publics. Such settings include national dance contests held throughout Ecuador and abroad, as well as job-related contexts in which both elites as well as tourist hotels specify their preference for bona-fide Quimseños employees (Crain 1996). The foregrounding of their dress, dance styles and 'folk' music as unique markers of Quimseño identity within intercultural settings is illuminated by Myers' (1994) analysis of the sand paintings that Australian aboriginal artists presented to a New York City gallery audience. Referring to the sand paintings created in the gallery, Myers (1994: 680) maintains that

> In recent years, and above all in western settings, aboriginal people are increasingly indexed by their artistic production, products that stand for their identity . . . [and] Aboriginal people have been participating increasingly as embodied representations of their cultural identity, displaying their culture in external contexts in the form of performance.
>
> (Myers 1994: 682)

The preceding portrait of *San Juan* as a transgressive space in which Quimseños exercise free reign in their inversion of elite codes must also be subject to qualification. The performances staged on indigenous terrain are not all of one piece. They make contradictory statements. On the one hand, the satisfying aesthetic performances of *San Juan* in Quimsa which they later tailor to suit the requirements of extra-local settings, such as in *La Casa de Cultura* (the 'National House of Culture') in Quito, an arena which formerly restricted the definition of 'culture' to performances of classical music, have strengthened their self-confidence. *Indígenas* realise that positive evaluations of their art by non-indigenous publics increases their symbolic capital as well as

their political leverage in external domains. However, these performances in *El Alto* also point to underlying conflicts. While the idiom of
fraternidad ('egalitarian brotherhood') guides much of ritualised
behaviour in *El Alto*, incipient hierarchies have also emerged, particularly during the post-agrarian reform period. Today not all families can
afford to be *priostes* of *San Juan*, and in comments voiced privately in
El Alto, particular kin groups who attain this position may be referred
to disparagingly as 'the new *patróns*', a term formerly used to designate
members of the dominant class. These hierarchies have been influenced
by migratory processes as well as a greater access to the market and
wage economy.

Prior to 1962, a peasant family who volunteered to be a *prioste*
needed a bountiful supply of grain and farm animals as well as the
collaboration of local kin to sponsor a successful *San Juan*. But by
1982, cash had become one of the most essential factors. Most cash
earnings for *San Juan* are generated by those Quimseños who have
emigrated to Quito, or abroad, or by *los hijos de los emigrantes* (the
emigrants' children). The latter groups may have spent most of their
lives outside of the community. Nevertheless the number of individuals
with some attachment to the community who do not return for *San
Juan* is extremely small. It is rumoured among the landed elite that
most Quimseños residing in Quito or beyond will go as far as to quit
their jobs if their employers do not grant a leave of absence to participate in the festivities. Such participation provides the perfect stage for
urban Quimseños to enact performances of their cultural difference
which reassert their membership in an indigenous community. This is
an identity which while often desired, is also increasingly required, as
only members of officially recognised indigenous communities can
qualify for access to many sources of national and international
funding. The preceding patterns account for the fact that many of the
most successful *priostes* in recent years have included Quimsa-based
families who have been able to mobilise a sizeable number of extra-
local kin. The former offer lodging, provide their home as a site for the
El Alto festivities and prepare the ceremonial foodstuffs and beverages
typical of *San Juan*, while other ritual expenses are absorbed by the
wage remittances contributed by their urban relatives.

Vignette two

Preparations for *San Juan* involving Quimseños as well as the
Rodríguez elites begin a full year in advance. On the last day of *San*

Juan during June 1982, those families who had decided to take on the costs of *prioste* for the following year approached the *patrón* and asked him for the gift of a rooster from the hacienda's *bodega* (storehouse). Following local custom, each *prioste* will return the rooster to the *patrón* twelvefold in the form of a tribute.

On the third day of *San Juan*, *indígenas* gather in *El Alto* at the homes of the different *priostes* bringing the twelve live roosters suspended on two branches which are draped across the sides of brightly decorated horses. Several other individuals carry household statues of St John which they hoist onto platforms on their shoulders. While Indian women dress in sumptuous festive apparel, the men's clothing ranges from velvet suit coats to finely woven ponchos. Men also wear the masked disguises and carry other ritual paraphernalia such as whips, in evidence in *El Alto*. Amidst an atmosphere of pageantry, each tributary party surrounds its horses and begins the procession through the streets towards the imposing gate of the hacienda.

Each *prioste* group enters the courtyard and proudly displays its regalia. High overhead, on the balcony of the manor house, are the *patrónes*, their personal servants consisting of *indígenas* as well as an eighty-year old wet-nurse born in Spain, and members of the extended Rodríguez family with their invited guests. While some of the elite have recently flown in from overseas destinations such as Paris, Milan, Miami and the Dominican Republic, others departed very early that same morning from Quito. In contrast to the majority of indigenous migrants who arrive by public transport, many of the Quito-based elites travel in their four-wheel-drive Nissan Patrols.

Below, scattered around the periphery of the courtyard, are mestizo families who reside in lower Quimsa, curious bystanders and foreign tourists. A few onlookers and tourists carry camcorders and begin to film this colourful event. Of all of the groups filling the courtyard, the mestizos are those most likely to covet spectator status, as this social location provides them with a respectable distance from what they regard as a disdainful 'indigenous ethnic performance'. As the crowd looks on, each *prioste* group approaches the balcony in succession, and a young boy on horseback praises the *patrón* by reciting a Biblical passage from St John. He then tosses one of the roosters to the *patrón*, and the latter rewards the best performer with the equivalent of US$2 in Ecuadorean currency.

Commentary on vignette two

Similar to the *San Juan* performances in *El Alto*, this second vignette is also traversed by internal fissures, as on occasion hierarchies and structural constraints are reinforced, while at other moments they are subverted. The vertical spatial arrangements, in which elites and their guests occupy the balcony above while *indígenas* occupy the courtyard below, inscribe deferential behaviour onto the body of the indigenous subject. Elite selves are constructed, and draw their power from their relationships to a surrogate Indian self. Initially, in the courtyard, many Quimseños adopt the 'image of the acquiescent Indian', a deferential role characteristic of the behaviour of the *indios propios*, who prior to agrarian reform were tied by debts to the estate. Such posturing facilitates employment opportunities for some Quimseños both at the Hacienda La Miranda and beyond. However, *indígenas* are not alone in negotiating their identities, as elites also engage in forms of 'impression-management' (Goffman 1959). *San Juan* is one of the rare periods during the year in which members of the entire Rodríguez family actually gather at the hacienda, and it is at this site that they assume diverse and often contradictory identities. Several members of the extended family either travel frequently, live abroad or study abroad, and only return 'home' at this time. Taking advantage of the presence of both the indigenous community and their own invited guests as well as a larger audience, many of the senior Rodríguez elites enact performances of *el buen patrón/la buena patrona* (the good landlord/landlady). By such a strategy they momentarily represent themselves as old-fashioned landlords who have not abandoned local traditions, while also gaining a certain degree of legitimacy for their otherwise contested monopolisation of vast extensions of parish land.

Later on the image of the deferential Indian is abruptly abandoned as Quimseños become brazen by assuming control of the courtyard. The multiplicity of their self-representations is suggested, as 'Indianness' shifts to become associated with disorder and boldness. Following the tribute of roosters to the landed elite, *indígenas* take the upper hand. Many ascend to the balcony of the hacienda, where they ply members of the Rodríguez family with *aguardiente* and tell them when it is time to return to the courtyard to dance their favourite contra-dances. Indigenous boldness and aggression, thought to be induced by ritual drinking during *San Juan*, has long disturbed agrarian elites. Displays both of real and potential violence still encountered in the post-agrarian reform period, are documented in earlier historical and ethnographic accounts.[9] In 1982, the owner of an estate bordering the Hacienda La Miranda who no longer co-sponsors *San Juan* with *indígenas* gave me his assessment of the ritual. His account was filled with a fear of Indian militancy:

> In *San Juan* the Indians come to me, and they say drink with us. And sometimes, there is no other choice than to drink with them. And the moment in which the Indian gets totally drunk his personality changes completely. He becomes aggressive and starts trouble.
>
> (Señor Ricardo Bartolomé,
> personal communication, 14 March 1982)

In 1992, other estate owners also described the potential dangers associated with indigenous behaviour during *San Juan*, such as instances of bodily injury, damage to farm machinery and the possibility of land invasions.

Vignette three: the elites' offstage performance

On 26 June 1983, I entered the hacienda courtyard with my neighbours and friends. Our entourage was led by Mama Juana Quintasama. The Quintasama's were an indigenous family who lived near the home of one of the seven sponsors of *San Juan* of 1983. Chatting with their group in the courtyard below, I was suprised to receive an impromptu invitation from Don Rodríguez asking me to join his guests for lunch. I had assumed that, as in the previous year, I would be spending my second *San Juan* in the company of this same Indian family.

Shortly after the Indians' tribute of roosters in the hacienda courtyard, members of the extended Rodríguez family retreat inside the mansion for an elaborate luncheon prepared for approximately thirty guests. The invited guests constituted a diverse group, including members of foreign diplomatic circles stationed in Ecuador (for example, I was sandwiched between the French and Spanish consuls), members of a United Nations development team, and foreign and Ecuadorean scholars.

In June 1992 I returned to Quimsa for *San Juan* and was again invited to join the Rodríguez elite for lunch. The group surrounding me was dressed casually, with Ralph Lauren polo shirts, imported designer jeans and Armani sunglasses everywhere in evidence. Many in this group had flown in from other destinations, in a similar manner that I had travelled to Quimsa from my home in Barcelona only a week before. Several of the invited guests were videotaping the *indígenas* circling the courtyard below. Through the clamour of Indian music, I caught snatches of conversations between family members and guests, ranging from a debate regarding the recent Cannes film festival to news of a business merger underway between an Ecuadorean and a Chilean firm. Members of the Rodríguez family initiated discussions with me, on topics that shifted from global to local themes. For example, Señor Rodríguez's son and his spouse told me about their recent trip to the World's Fair in Seville. Directly following their account, two of the Rodríguez sisters expressed their desire to learn more about an aspect of life in *El Alto* which, in their social position as elites, remained off-limits to them. Upon being informed of my professional identity as an anthropologist, they quizzed me regarding the charade-like games played by *indígenas* at 3 a.m. during *velorios* (wakes for the dead), which follow intense periods of grieving.

Commentary on vignette three

While I had daily contacts with *indígenas* as a result of in-depth participant-observation and the sharing of meals and festive occasions, my encounters with members of the Rodríguez family had always been less frequent. It was not so easy for me to keep up with the lifestyle and mobility of this transnational family, nor was it always easy to convince the Rodríguez elites to discuss certain issues with me. Many of my encounters with this family had taken the form of highly structured interviews, typically in Quito, and occasionally at the rural hacienda, and in both contexts time was usually a constraining factor. This lack of everyday interaction provided me with a good reason to accept the lunch invitation. To a much greater degree than in the case of the *indígenas*, I had acquired knowledge regarding the Rodríguez family's diverse identities through mass-mediated forms of representation such as a television documentary and radio, newspaper and literary accounts. For example, I will never forget the shock I experienced one evening during 1982 when I recognised the voice of one member of the Rodríguez family entering my 'home' in *El Alto* via an international media forum emanating from my country of birth. This experience challenged basic assumptions that informed the core of my earlier professional training. It made me question the degree to which I needed to leave my North American 'home' in order to do 'fieldwork'.

From our luncheon conversations in the courtyard, it became apparent that St John provided many of the invited guests with an 'insider's backstage view' of indigenous culture, while also serving to consolidate their cosmopolitan identities. Our menu consisted of a sampling of indigenous dishes such as *sopa de quinoa* (quinoa soup), *mondongo* (tripe pudding) and *humitas* (cornbread steamed in a folded leaf) as well as other favourites such as strip steak, followed by artesanal ice-cream and chocolate cakes which appealed to an international palate. These festivities enhanced the prestige both of the Rodríguez elites, and by association their estate, the Hacienda La Miranda, as this well maintained colonial mansion has acquired the status of an international showcase as well as a hands-on ethnic museum. This status was highlighted as early as the 1960s when the *San Juan* fiesta, but only that portion celebrated in the hacienda courtyard, was featured in an issue of *National Geographic*. During the first half of the 1960s, only members of an eminent Ecuadorean elite family (and not indigenous peasants) possessed the symbolic capital necessary to attract international media attention. Media images of this portion of *San Juan* which reproduce the hacienda as a site entice new audiences, as diverse publics want to be where a media event has occurred and might possibly happen again. For many of the sophisticated urbanites who were present during the 1982 luncheon, the performance of this seemingly 'timeless' rural tradition in the ancient stone courtyard conveyed a sense of 'imperialist nostalgia', by creating a longing for a world of colonial relations in which landlord–peasant ties were imagined to have been more harmonious (Rosaldo 1989).

However, if I juxtaposed the preceding impressions alongside my ethnographic findings from working among *indígenas*, I knew that many of the latter could not share the impressions which this occasion elicited for the elites. For example, in the context of a series of political assemblies held in *El Alto* during 1982–4 in which elites were not present, I had heard Quimseños (both more permanent community residents as well as migrants) engaged in heated discussions regarding a possible 'museumification' of the Hacienda La Miranda. These dialogues were interspersed with rumours that such a project could occur in the near future, if 'national patrimony legislation' was implemented at the Hacienda La Miranda. The National Institute of Cultural Patrimony is dedicated to the discovery, restoration and preservation of properties which form part of 'the public trust' of Ecuador (Bommes and Wright 1982). According to the national decree of June 1979 which established it, the Institute is charged with the conservation of 'a diverse array of creations realised by the Ecuadorean *pueblo* [people] during the long course of their history'. It includes 'archaeological remains, temples, convents, chapels, colonial buildings . . . maps . . . documents related to Ecuadorean independence from Spain and ethnographic objects of scientific, historical or artistic value' (*El Comercio* 1980: 12). The negative implications of this legislation seemed apparent to those Quimseños who attended the assemblies. Many argued that the National Patrimony's definition of 'the Ecuadorean *pueblo*' had been formulated by professional experts, and the latter would not acknowledge indigenous peoples' opinions regarding objects which are of either historical or artistic value. Others claimed that if the Hacienda La Miranda was declared national patrimony, it would be placed under the jurisdiction of the Ecuadorean government and perhaps be displayed for the purposes of historical tourism. There was a general feeling that implementation of this legislation would leave Quimseños with little chance that their own ancestral claims to what the Ecuadorean state currently regards as 'hacienda land' would ever be recognised.[10]

Similar to the performances staged by Quimseños in the courtyard, *San Juan* is a highly visible occasion in which the Rodríguez elites also fashion diverse representations of self which foreground their uniqueness. This celebration attracts an audience which authenticates, and media technologies which disseminate images of *indígenas* engagements with elites. While the Rodríguez elites initially construct their identities in relation to negative representations of 'Indianness', this is quickly altered as they incorporate images of Indian difference as part of their own global construction of self. The latter identity is a product both of elite self-creation within this particular context, as well as of shifting political, economic and cultural discourses emerging during the past two decades, both in Ecuador and abroad, which have begun to call into question the Rodríguez elites' dominant positioning relative to the *indígenas*. For example, a new innovation occurred during 1992. Several female elites began to appropriate signs of indigenous identity, combining these with elements drawn from a global consumer culture. For example, Doña Carmina Rodríguez, a senior member of the rural aristocracy, combined a 1950s vintage-style skirt which she had recently bought in Italy with an elaborately embroidered Quimseña blouse purchased from an Indian woman. Having recently returned from visiting relatives in Paris, Doña Carmina explained to me that she felt equally 'at home' in France and in Quimsa. As if to prove her point, she readily descended to the courtyard to indicate her dual affiliations, by dancing and drinking with the *indígenas*. Elite appropriation of the signifiers of 'Indianness' has also occurred in urban Quito. During the past ten years, young women of the Rodríguez family have conveyed an 'ethnic look' by introducing *shigras* (bags of woven cactus fibre) produced by indigenous women as part of their everyday street wear. Such a practice has increased the demand for these bags both among middle-class Ecuadorean women as well as foreign tourists, and it has also augmented the export of these artisanal products abroad.

If they presently maintain a relatively privileged position *vis-à-vis* Quimseños, why would the Rodríguez elites want to reconfigure their identities as *indígenas*? At this point I can only suggest a few tentative answers which depart from a more locally oriented interpretation of this event as the repetition of 'a seemingly anachronistic traditional ritual of inversion'. As mentioned previously, the Rodríguez elites' involvement in a late twentieth-century cultural economy which traffics in signs that express novelty, is one factor generating these new self-images. Furthermore, as very globally oriented elites, members of this family are aware of ongoing 'nativist' and fourth-world peoples' political movements occurring in other parts of the world today. They can imagine a transformation of present social locations, and to a certain degree, during *San Juan*, the Rodríguez elites experience this transformation on a symbolic level.

Knowledge of subtle changes in their privileged position with respect to indigenous peoples can be detected in the small jokes made by members of the Rodríguez family, such as the one about standing in line at the Hertz car rental agency in Miami airport, only to discover that some six textile-laden Otavaleños (Quimsa's indigenous neighbors) had just hired the last model of the car they had hoped to rent. The former are quite conscious that Quimseños, although presently deterritorialised, are implicated both in movements of reterritorialisation as well as in alternative projects which demand respect for indigenous cultural differences. By 1986, CONAIE, la Confederación de Nacionalidades Indígenas del Ecuador (Confederation of Indigenous Nationalities of Ecuador) emerged as an influential political force on the national stage. While not rejecting the legitimacy of the Ecuadorean state, this confederation has attempted to refashion the meaning of 'the nation' for *indígenas*, and it has gained numerous concessions. It has argued for further attention to indigenous land claims and a greater degree of political autonomy for the respective native groups. Later, in June 1990, *el Levantamiento Indígena* (the

Indigenous Uprising) invaded public spaces. Indigenous groups block-aded the Pan-American highway in order to keep peasant produce from reaching urban markets, and organised sit-ins in government ministries (Zamosc 1994). Finally, the Ecuadorean government has placed a large portion of territory in Ecuador's oil-rich eastern lowlands under indigenous control. In the aftermath of lowlanders' successful resolution of their territorial demands, a range of Quimseños (local residents and returned migrants as well as migrants residing in Quito and abroad) have become increasingly involved in litigation to restore their ancestral claims to land.[11] Today many receive a modicum of legal protection, whereas prior to 1962 a hacienda owner could summon the military to take the *indígenas* to jail, even for minor infractions. As was the case during my earlier field research in 1982–4, *indígenas* expect anthropologists who reside in their community to take a stand and assist them both with their land-claim suits and with related efforts such as their fight for reforms within the national educational system (Crain 1989, 1994).

In the public culture of the new 'pluri-ethnic Ecuadorean state', *indígenas* are increasingly recognised as political actors. In contrast to some two decades ago, members of indigenous groups now appear on national television addressing the viewing public both in Quichua as well as in Spanish; they are elected to lower-level political offices; and many have found employment in government ministries. They are also courted by foreign NGOs (non-governmental organisations) which have provided them with access to new sources of power that transcend the realm of the Ecuadorean state. Several indigenous leaders from Quimsa have travelled abroad, to assert their cultural and political claims as well as to promote their commerce. They presently move in those very same international circles which were once the quasi-private reserve of Ecuador's elite. Aware of external discourses regarding intellectual property rights as well as ecological issues, Quimseños have entered dialogues with the members of pan-Andean coalitions. Quimseños increasingly refer to themselves in international forums as the guardians of Ecuador's pre-Colombian heritage, as ecologically correct managers of Andean resources and as the only legitimate owners of Andean territory. As the elites' monopolisation of both national as well as transnational symbol-making loses its hege-monic hold, and they can no longer speak so convincingly for indigenous peoples, they strive to recuperate their dominant position in public spaces. Elite appropriation of the signs of 'Indianness' in contexts as diverse as the Hacienda La Miranda and urban Quito, constitutes an attempt to reassert such control.

Concluding remarks

Where is 'the field'? And where is that place in which we may ground our identities, in a globalised, deterritorialised world? *Indígenas* experiences of *San Juan*, as well as those of elites and my own, surpassed the space delimited by the rural community of Quimsa and the Hacienda La Miranda. Analysis of *San Juan* provides a critical reappraisal of notions such as 'community', 'place' and 'stable, unitary identities', which formed the conceptual basis of many case studies in earlier ethnographic analysis. By exploring 'processes of place-making' in relation to practices of identity politics, we see that actors drawn from metropolitan cultural centres such as Quito, Paris, Barcelona, La Paz and Washington DC played a crucial role both in constructing and in narrating the production of this event. Displacements of contemporary populations, the result of voluntary travel, political and economic diasporas, and an influx of global commodities and new media, create conditions which have revitalised the celebration of *San Juan* during the post-agrarian reform period. However, as 'communities' and 'localities' are increasingly produced by global processes and imagined via diverse forms of media representation, what was once a pre-Hispanic celebration of the sun, and some four decades ago a hierarchical ritual celebrating landed elite–indigenous peasant relations, now serves as a space both for cosmopolitan elites as well as globally savvy *indígenas* to construct globally informed political statements about their identities.

The performative analogy informing this chapter illuminates issues both of identity construction and of place-making. Considered as a series of vignettes, *San Juan* and its performances provide arenas for *indígenas* and the Rodríguez elites to project new identities and negotiate former ones that are witnessed by a diverse viewing public. Analysis of a range of elite performative behaviours held in intercultural interactions in the hacienda courtyard, and later in the offstage luncheon, demonstrates the manner in which the Rodríguez elites have appropriated signs of 'Indianness' as strategies to bolster their weakening hegemony. In both of these settings they have conveyed images of selfhood which carry 'indigenous' and 'ethnic' inflections. However, the increasing visibility of the *indígenas* in national arenas and abroad has de-centred the elites' unique role as the culture-makers.[12] As identities are constructed relationally and on a shifting terrain, positive evaluations of their cultural performances to non-indigenous publics have encouraged Quimsa *indígenas* to essentialise their identities by feeding these external desires for cultural difference. Returning annually to create 'authentic Indianness' in the hacienda courtyard, Quimseños performances of unique visual and acoustic displays remind diverse constituencies that their land ownership claims are enveloped in broader cultural and historical debates, and that these claims remain a contested issue, in the parish, today. While the Rodríguez elites travel to the *San Juan* celebration to put on native dress and serve indigenous foods to their guests, many *indígenas* shed their western dress, don 'native trappings' and journey to *San Juan* in order to cash in on their 'cultural difference' and ethnic identity during a period in which 'difference' is so highly valued in other cosmopolitan fields beyond Quimsa.

Notes

1 Acknowledgements: The research which forms the basis of this chapter was conducted for twenty-four months from 1982–4 and for six months during 1992, and was funded by the American Council for Learned Societies, and the Henry and Grace Doherty Foundation at Princeton University. Much shorter versions of this article were delivered in the 'Moving Frontiers' workshop convened by Joan Pujadas during the EASA congress of 1996, and in the 'Morals and the Margins' workshop convened by João Pina-Cabral and Thomas Hylland Eriksen for the EASA congress of 1994. I thank Manuel Delfino and Felicia Hughes-Freeland for their insights, critical commentary and technical support. I would also like to acknowledge the assistance of Karsten Paerregaard, whose tapas-inspired conversation provoked a further reconceptualisation of the arguments outlined here.

2 The following literature illustrates this argument (see Hannerz 1987; Appadurai 1991, Rouse 1991; Crain 1992, 1997; Gupta and Ferguson 1992, 1997; Malkii 1997).

3 While acknowledging processes of hybridity, I am not dismissing the . importance of practices of 'strategic essentialism' which many minority groups must deploy to ensure their survival in contexts in which their voices, rights and/or resources would otherwise be subject to erasure. For further discussion of this point see Spivak 1993; Crain 1996; Lavie and Swedenburg 1996.

4 Several authors have suggested that *San Juan* coincided with the pre-Hispanic festival of the sun known among the Inca as *Inti-Raymi* (see Parsons 1945; Crespi 1981).

5 *Indígena* is a social construct which is the product of a positive ethnic identity which Quimseños claimed for themselves following the agrarian reform, as indigenous peasants emigrated from the community and were increasingly subject to being classified as 'other', and therefore different.

6 In the aftermath of Quimsa's agrarian reform, the Hacienda La Miranda only employs 10 per cent of its former labour force. For further information see Crain 1989.

7 Many, but not all of the homes of the indigenous peasantry have *santos*. These are taken before the fiesta of the patron saint to be blessed by a priest in either the hacienda chapel or the parish church (located in a nearby community). By 1983, many Quimseños wanted to construct a community-based church that would free their religious practices from any unnecessary involvement with either the hacienda chapel or the parish church.

8 Earlier ethnographies as well as travellers' accounts provide evidence of these innovations (see Parsons 1945; Haussarek 1967; Crespi 1981).

9 Written accounts of group confrontations have alluded to two distinct forms encountered during the climax of *San Juan*. First, there are accounts of aggressive 'ritual battles' between *indígenas* and elites and/or other authority figures (the military, the police) occurring within the courtyard of particular haciendas. There are also accounts which refer to groups of *indígenas* from different *parcialidades* (territories within a specific community) who engage in these 'battles' with one another in the public plazas of nearby communities. For further information regarding these cases, see Parsons 1945; Haussarek 1967).

10 The construction of the past favoured by the Ecuadorean national patrimony lobby produces a view of history that conceals the conflicting relationships engendered by colonialism and the subsequent era, in which the large landed estates have emerged, and continue to exist, only as a result of the expropriation of Indian communal lands.

11 During the first year in which I resided in Quimsa the *Jefe de Cabildo* (the popularly elected head of the community governing council) was a Quimsa migrant based in Quito. He commuted to the capital for employment from Monday through Friday and returned 'home' each weekend to join his wife and children. Many Quimseños explained that 'this arrangement' was not a handicap, as his residence in Quito allowed him to take care of community related paper work, such as land claims, in the government ministries.

12 The following case provides one example of successful *indígenas* performances abroad. Andean musicians (heterogeneous groups with members from Bolivia, Ecuador and Peru) draw large crowds in Barcelona's largest and most frequented public space, the Plaça de Catalunya. As street musicians, they have acquired 'de facto' control over a particular corner of this space. While performing for free, they pass a hat round for contributions and peddle their compact discs.

Bibliography

Appadurai, A. (1991) 'Global Ethnoscapes: Notes and Queries for a Transnational Anthropology', in R. Fox (ed.) *Recapturing Anthropology: Working in the Present*, Santa Fe NM: School of American Research Press.

Bell, C. (1992) *Ritual Theory, Ritual Practice*, Oxford: Oxford University Press.

Boissevain, J. (ed.) (1992) Introduction to *Revitalising European Rituals*, London: Routledge.

Bommes, M. and Wright, P. (1982) ' "Charms of residence": The Public and the Past', in R. Johnson, G. McLennan, B. Schwartz and D. Sutton (eds) *Making Histories: Studies in History-Writing and Politics*, Birmingham: Centre for Contemporary Cultural Studies.

Buitrón, A. (1964) 'La Fiesta de San Juan en Otavalo', in P. de Carvalho-Neto (ed.) *Antologia del Folklore Ecuatoriana*, vol. 2, Quito: Editorial Universitaria.

Clifford, J. (1997) *Routes: Travel and Translation in the Late Twentieth Century*, Cambridge MA: Harvard University Press.

Crain, M. M. (1989) *Ritual, Memoria Popular y El Proceso Politíco en la Sierra Ecuatoriana*, Quito: Abya Yala Press and Corporacíon Editora Nacional.

——(1990) 'The Social Construction of National Identity in Highland Ecuador', *Anthropological Quarterly*, 63, 1: 43–59.

——(1991) 'Women's Narratives of Death and Devil Possession in the Ecuadorean Andes', *American Ethnologist*, 18, 1: 67–89.

——(1992) 'Pilgrims, Yuppies and Media-men: The Transformation of an Andalusian Pilgrimage', in J. Boissevain (ed.) *Revitalising European Rituals*, London: Routledge.

——(1994) 'Unruly Mothers: Gender Identities, Political Discourses and Struggles for Social Space in the Ecuadorean Andes', *Political and Legal Anthropology Review*, 15, 2: 98–110.

——(1996) 'The Gendering of Ethnicity in the Ecuadorean Highlands: Native Womens' Self-fashioning in the Urban Marketplace', in M. Melhuus and K. A. Stølen (eds) *Machos, Mistresses and Madonnas: Contesting the Power of Latin American Gender Imagery*, London: Verso.

——(1997) 'From Local Cult of the Virgin to Media Rite: The Cultural Politics of Transformation and Visual Representation in an Andalusian Romería', in A. Gupta and J. Ferguson (eds) *Culture, Power, Place: Explorations in a Critical Anthropology*, Durham NC: Duke University Press.

Crespi, M. (1981) 'St John the Baptist: The Ritual Looking Glass of Hacienda-Indian Ethnic and Power Relations', in N. E. Whitten Jr (ed.) *Cultural Transformations and Ethnicity in Modern Ecuador*, Champaign-Urbana IL: University of Illinois Press.

Dubisch, J. (1995) *In a Different Place: Gender, Politics and Pilgrimage at a Greek Island Shrine*, Princeton NJ: Princeton University Press.

Eade, J. and Sallnow, M. (eds) (1991) Introduction to *Contesting the Sacred: The Anthropology of Christian Pilgrimage*, London: Routledge.

El Comercio (1980) 'El Instituto Nacional de Patrimonio Cultural: Salvemos lo Nuestro', 5 October, Sunday supplement, 12.

Fernandez, J. (1986) *Persuasions and Performances: The Play of Tropes in Culture*, Bloomington IN: Indiana University Press.

Goffman, E. (1959) *The Presentation of Self in Everyday Life*, Harmondsworth: Penguin Books.

Gupta, A. and Ferguson, J. (1992) 'Beyond Culture: Space, Identity and the Politics of Difference', *Cultural Anthropology*, 7, 1: 6–23.

Gupta, A. and Ferguson, J. (eds) (1997) Introduction to *Culture, Power, Place: Explorations in a Critical Anthropology*, Durham NC: Duke University Press.

Hannerz, U. (1987) 'The World in Creolization', *Africa*, 57, 4: 546–59.

——(1989) 'Notes on the Cultural Ecumene', *Public Culture*, 1, 2: 66–75.

——(1990) 'Cosmopolitans and Locals in World Culture', *Theory, Culture & Society*, 7: 237–51.

Haussarek, F. (1967) [1868] *Four Years Among the Ecuadorians*, Latin American travel series, Carbondale IL: Southern Illinois University Press.

Howes, D. (ed.) (1996) Introduction to *Cross-Cultural Consumption*, New York: Routledge.

Hughes-Freeland, F. (ed.) (1998) Introduction to *Ritual, Performance, Media*, London: Routledge.

Kane, S. (1994) *The Phantom Gringo Boat: Shamanic Discourse and the Politics of Development in Panama*, Washington: Smithsonian Institute Press.

Lavie, S. and Swedenburg, T. (eds) (1996) Introduction to *Displacement, Diaspora and the Geographies of Identity*, Durham NC: Duke University Press.

Lavie, S., Narayan, K. and Rosaldo, R. (eds) (1993) *Creativity/Anthropology*, Ithaca NY: Cornell University Press.

MacAloon, J. (ed.) (1984) Introduction to *Rite, Drama, Festival, Spectacle: Rehearsals Towards a Theory of Performance*, Philadelphia PA: Institute for the Study of Human Issues.

Malkii, L. (1997) 'National Geographic: The Rooting of Peoples and the Territorialization of National Identity among Scholars and Refugees', in A. Gupta and J. Ferguson (eds) *Culture, Power, Place: Explorations in a Critical Anthropology*, Durham NC: Duke University Press.

Myers, F. (1994) 'Culture-Making: Performing Aboriginality at the Asia Society Gallery', *American Ethnologist*, 21, 4: 679–99.

Paerregaard, K. (1997) 'Imagining a Place in the Andes: In the Borderland of Lived, Invented and Analysed Culture', in K. Fog Olwig and K. Hastrup (eds) *Siting Culture: The Shifting Anthropological Object*, London: Routledge.

Parsons, E. C. (1945) *Peguche: A Study of Andean Indians*, Chicago IL: University of Chicago Press.

Rosaldo, R. (1989) *Culture and Truth: The Remaking of Social Analysis*, Boston MA: Beacon Press.

Rouse, R. (1991) 'Mexican Migration and the Social Space of Postmodernism', *Diaspora*, 1, 1: 8–23.

——(1995) 'Questions of Identity: Personhood and Collectivity in Transnational Migration to the United States', *Critique of Anthropology*, 15: 350–80.

Schechner, R. (1992) *The Future of Ritual: Writings on Culture and Performance*, London: Routledge.

Schechner, R. and Appel, W. (1990) *By Means of Performance: Intercultural Studies of Theatre and Ritual*, Cambridge: Cambridge University Press.

Schieffelin, E. (1985) 'Performance and the Cultural Construction of Reality', *American Ethnologist*, 12, 4: 707–24.

Spivak, G. (1993) *Outside in the Teaching Machine*, New York: Routledge.

Taussig, M. (1993) *Mimesis and Alterity: A Particular History of the Senses*, London: Routledge.

Taylor, J. (1982) 'The Politics of Aesthetic Debate: The Case of Brazilian Carnival', *Cultural Anthropology*, 21: 301–12.

Wolf, E. W. (1982) *Europe and the People Without History*, Berkeley CA: University of California Press.

Zamosc, L. (1994) 'Agrarian Protest and the Indian Movement in the Ecuadorian Highlands', *Latin American Research Review*, 29, 3: 37–68.

Index